TALES OF YORE

VOLUME 1: STORIES FROM GREEK AND ROMAN MYTHS

DR U. FATHIMA FARZANA

Made with ♥ on the Notion Press Platform
www.notionpress.com

to mom & dad

Contents

Contents

Contents

CHAPTER ONE

Introduction

Note: This "Introduction" should be read after you've completed the tales. The essence of the myths is more important than any scholarly piece of writing on them. This provides additional information and helps those who are interested in classical research.

Myths are as vast as the expanding universe and it is a hard task to introduce the reader to mythology. These are not just tales to be told for entertainment but these served as the texts of the major religion of Greece followed for more than a thousand years. Labelled today as Paganism, the religion of ancient Greece and Rome gave birth to some of the best classics like the *Iliad* and the *Odyssey* (700 BCE) that have stood the test of time. These myths have changed the course of history and given us some of the best books ever written. The modern reader must understand that there is no 'one' single book for these myths. Their origins span across centuries before the birth of Christ over vast islands across the Mediterranean.

These myths were part of an oral tradition and sung in the castles of kings or recited on battlefields to encourage the warriors. That is why many of the heroes in these tales are descendants of gods and goddesses and the participants themselves are further heirs of these heroes. So a recitation of the heroic deeds of your ancestors will surely motivate you, won't it, especially if a bard of royal lineage says you are from the line of Achilles or Hercules? And Homer is neither the beginning nor the prominent of all these sources. Much of the narrative for the tales in this book is sourced from mainstream authors such as Ovid, Hesiod, Homer, Sappho, Herodotus and Virgil. I call them 'mainstream' because their texts share similarities and complement each other. Moreover, the texts of these authors are easily available to the modern reader. But of course, there are plenty of other sources that are not as prominent. For instance, in this "Introduction," I have made use of variations from Apollodorus' *Bibliotheque* 'The Library of Greek Mythology'. This is because I wanted to include some additional details which lead to a better understanding of these myths. And of course, to add a touch of surprise. There are sources such as the *Homeric Hymns*, *Argonautica*, *Little Iliad*, *Aithipia*, *De Divinatione* and the *Pythian Odes* written in different centuries. But for clarity's sake, I have used the sources of the mainstream authors in these tales.

All of these myths centre around a hero who has to take a quest. At the end of his quest, the hero either emerges transformed for the better or dies a tragic death paving the way for better people to do his duties. There were many heroes before Achilles and Paris was not the first to abduct the beautiful Helen of Troy. Surprisingly, Helen was also not the first princess to be abducted for a political vantage. Would you be taken aback when I tell you that the famed "Trojan Horse" never appears in the *Iliad*? Virgil and Pseudo-Apollodorus (he will be mentioned as Apollodorus in this book to prevent confusion) present different versions of it. Virgil gives the credit of the horse to Odysseus while Apollodorus gives it to Epius. Homer's *Iliad* ends with the death of Hector and never mentions anything about the death of Achilles.

The Greeks were not the first ones to siege Troy either. And Achilles was not dipped in Styx nor did he have any divine powers. If you have read the poem "Musée des Beaux Arts" by W. H. Auden, you might've felt sorry for Daedalus weeping over Icarus. However, if you read the life of Daedalus in Athens, you will get to know his dark secrets. He lost his son because he had committed murder. The purpose of these tales is to lay down plain old facts as they appear in the classics, stripped bare of the ornamentation added by media and the recent recreations of myths by authors like Rick Riordan. If you like *Percy Jackson and the Lightning Thief*, you may like it better after reading the real myth of Perseus.

Greek and Roman myths can be classified into two major fields for our better understanding - i) The Realm of Gods and ii) The Realm of Men. The creation myth [refer to Appendix 2] from Hesiod's *Theogony* (700 BCE), tales of gods, goddesses and monsters all belong to the former category. Tales of heroic kings, valiant heroes like Achilles, Hercules and even ordinary people like Baucis and Philemon belong to the latter. Mt. Olympus was the heavenly abode of the gods, Earth or Gaia was where men lived and the Underworld was the realm of the dead. Zeus ruled Mt. Olympus and watched over both gods [refer to Appendix 1] and men. Hades was king of the Underworld and ruled over the dead. Earth was a morphing zone where different gods claimed dominion over different elements and sometimes even fought with men. For instance, Ovid subtly hints at the anger and vengeance of Athena and

Poseidon in their clash to be nominated as the chief deity of Athens.

There are, however, various complex themes underlying these myths and these are explained for the uninitiated reader in the next few pages. And many of these are from the cultural and geographical setup of Greece. This book is built upon the structure offered by Ovid in his *Metamorphoses*. Homer's epics are placed last because those of Perseus, Hercules, Theseus and Jason precede Homeric heroes. I have stuck to only the descriptions and facts mentioned in the classics. The conversations between various characters in this book are adapted from the epics. The glossary and appendices will provide additional information wherever required.

1. The Deluge

Zeus had created the first humans from his precious ichor (blood of the gods) but he was quite dissatisfied with them. The Bronze Age men were particularly annoying as they had neither fear nor respect for the gods. They were a war-mongering race who always lusted for wealth and power. Zeus had been irritated by Lycaon, Tyrant of Arcadia. Lycaon wanted to find out if Zeus was indeed a god and invited him for a feast. The furious king ordered his servants to slaughter and cook a hostage for the meal. Of course, Zeus found the foul truth and Lycaon did not stop at that. He tried to murder Zeus to find out if he was truly immortal. Furious, Zeus struck Arcadia with a thunderbolt and transformed Lycaon and his sons into wolves. Lycaon is the first human to be transformed as mentioned by Ovid in Book 1 of the *Metamorphosis* (AD 8). This is indeed the earliest Greek evidence of werewolves. Hence the term lycanthropy (lupus = wolf) has come into existence.

Enraged by the lack of respect, Zeus returned to Mt. Olympus and called a council of the gods. Many of the gods were worried that their temples and altars would be empty without humans. Who would bring them offerings? Who would tend their flames and sacrifice in their names? Zeus announced his master plan. He would make a second set of humans; this time from stone. He would not repeat the same mistake of using his ichor again. He unlocked the clouds and released the winds. A colossal flood washed away all life from the face of the earth. Those who survived the flood died of starvation. Deucalion (the son of Prometheus and Asia) and his wife Pyrrha were the only survivors who would soon create the next generation of humans.

What is surprising is that the deluge myth a.k.a the precursor for the creation myth occurs in quite a few sources much before the Bible. The very first deluge myth appears in the *Epic of Gilgamesh* (2000 BCE?) where the wise Utanapishti narrates it to the hero Gilgamesh. Apparently, Utanapishti and his wife are of a higher descent - just like Deucalion and Pyrrha - and remain the only survivors of a flood. The god Ea appears to Utanapishti and advises him to construct a boat. This is how the wise man and his wife survive. Plato's lesser-known dialogue *Timaeus* (350 BCE?) is the next source of a deluge myth where Zeus destroys the first humans. But Prometheus overhears the god's plan and advises his brother Deucalion to escape. However, in Ovid's *Metamorphosis*, Deucalion is chosen by Zeus to create the next generation of men.

1. **The Virgin Goddesses - Athena, Artemis, Hestia**

"Virgin" actually meant "an independent woman" or "a woman without a man" in ancient times. The meaning changed to "a chaste woman" or "a pure woman" only during the Mediaeval period when writers and artists recreated Christian art from Greek myths. Gilgamesh was the first virgin-born prince of Sumeria. He was a demi-god and had superhuman strength. Many goddesses were hailed as virgins in those days - Isis, Hathor, Athena, Ishtar and Astarte - to name a few. All of them had sexual relations and even children.

Athena's adopted son Erichthonius became the legendary ruler of Greece. He is said to be the second virgin-born prince in world myth. Goddesses like Athena, Artemis and Hestia lived independently like men and so they were virgins. According to Apollodorus, Athena was the only one among the Olympians who could hurl Zeus' thunderbolt. When Aias tries to return from the Trojan War without sacrificing to the gods, "Athena hurled a thunderbolt at the ship of Aias" (262). Fighting, hunting and guarding homesteads were the least likely of feminine duties and so the goddesses who watched over these were virgins indeed. They could be very well called the first independent career women in world literature. Heroes who went into battle often called them for victory and the lucky hunter was indeed lucky only if the goddess chose him.

Artemis was the goddess of the hunt; the daughter of Zeus and Latona. She was Apollo's twin sister. She was often accompanied by young maidens and nymphs. Artemis was said to be the protectress of young maidens and hunters. She was depicted with a bow and a quiver full of arrows. She was a vengeful goddess who turned Calydon to stone for spying on her while she was bathing. Artemis also assisted many heroes like Orion who she turned into a constellation. Artemis is depicted living alone and independent much like Athena.

Hestia was the goddess of the hearth; daughter of Cronos and sister of Zeus. Feasts were opened with an offering to Hestia. She was chief of the goddesses and maintained the hearth fire of Olympus. Young maidens called Vestal Virgins served her altar. As the title indicates, these women remained celibate during their servitude. Aphrodite is said to have no power over Hestia and the charms of Cupid failed on her. Such was her independence and personal power.

3. **Women in Greek Mythology - wife/virgin, witch or warrior**

Women characters, both divine and mortal, appear to have pretty much the same traits in Greek mythology. They can be placed in three categories

i) virgin or wife - Helen of Troy, Queen Niobe, Daphne, Danaë, Semele, Andromeda, Arachne, Myrrha and every other 'domestic' maiden/princess/queen belongs to this category. These women appear pretty much helpless and so become victims of abuse, rape, incest or vengeance of the gods. Even the daughters of goddesses like Persephone belong to this group. The presence of these women shows domestic simplicity and the duties of the household. Or, in the case of victims, they represent innocence and purity. It is very evident that the innocent Polyxena is used to show female modesty in the face of death. Though Polyxena was sacrificed by Neoptolemus before the tomb of Achilles, she gathered her clothes around her and preserved her modesty till the very end. Other minor characters like nymphs - Echo, for instance - stand for nature destroyed by humans. These nymphs and nature spirits could very well be the first elements of ecocriticism observed in myth.

ii) witch or sorceress - Pasiphaë, Circe, Medea and Calypso remain the most powerful women who changed the course of myth itself. Jason would not have succeeded in the trials of Aeetes if not for Medea. Bacchus himself got a wish granted by Medea. Circe could transform people into beasts. Apollodorus records that Circe could change men into "wolves, and others into pigs, or asses, or lions" (272). She also made a stingray-tipped spear for her son Telegonos who was born to Odysseus. It was with this weapon that Odysseus' life came to an end. Calypso could hypnotise people to do whatever she wanted. Pasiphaë was the wife of Minos and the queen of Crete. She had a cult of her own. All these women were exceedingly intelligent and the heroes depended upon their powers and their counsel. They appear as key narrative markers who provide valuable information on the hero's quest. Their magic is often connected with nature as they were also herbalists.

iii) warrior - Atalanta, Deianira, Penthesileia, Hippolyta and the Amazons were warriors and efficient rulers who often fought alongside heroes. These women could be the very first feminist representations of women. Apollodorus presents Deianeira, the last wife of Hercules, as a woman who "drove a chariot and practised the arts of war" (93). Atalanta was the first to shoot and pierce the Calydonian boar. The other Atalanta (wife of Hippomenes) was swift-footed and raced the heroes. Penthesileia is the only one to make Achilles break a sweat. These warrior women were independent, powerful and strong but they lacked the intelligence of the witches. For that reason, they were soon victimised or killed. They represented the Earth at its finest, fighting but giving up to men.

4. Homosexuality in myth - Narcissus, Hyacinthus, Achilles and Cyparissus

Homosexuality is a recurrent theme and Zeus himself is said to have preferred the beautiful Ganymede to all his female consorts. Narcissus fell in love with himself, Hyacinthus was beloved of Apollo, Patroclus was loved by Achilles and Cyparissus was yet another of Apollo's love interests. This homosexuality is based on the ancient Greek custom of pederasty where a young adolescent boy was entrusted to an older man to learn the ways of life. According to these ancient Greeks, the younger partner was often effeminate and so the relationship was not considered homosexual or taboo. These relationships were temporary and both the partners had female consorts as well. The same could be said of women who also felt the need for younger companions of the same sex. Saphho's poems are addressed to younger women, praising their sexual beauty and love. These relationships were also temporary and not considered homosexual.

5. Rape and incest

Rape is a common recurring theme in Greek mythology. Most of the transformations in Ovid's *Metamorphoses* are results of rape. Zeus, Poseidon, Apollo and Hades rape mortal women. Many of the heroes - Perseus, Hercules and Theseus - are children born to rape victims. Helen of Troy was born to Leda raped by Zeus. Apollodorus states that Helen was born to Zeus and Nemesis, the goddess of vengeance. Nemesis, raped by Zeus, had laid an egg in the woods which was brought to Leda by a shepherd. When the egg hatched and Helen stepped out, Leda raised her as her own. It was also the will of Zeus "so that his daughter would become famous for having brought Europe and Asia to war, or, as others have said, to ensure that the race of demigods would be raised to glory" (243). But the fact is that these 'victims' are not victims in the sense they don't feel violated. Those who accept give birth to heroes and demigods. Those who resist end up as monsters like Medusa or inanimate beings like Daphne. It can be noted that the gods take up the forms of beasts or inanimate objects before they rape mortal women. Zeus appears as a swan before Leda, a shower of gold for Danaë and a bull for Europa. However, these 'rapes' are not considered acts of injustice or violence, not by the victims or the writers who narrate their tales.

Mortal men who rape innocent women are quickly disposed of. These men become icons of disgrace and their victims take vengeance upon them. Philomela and Procne repay Tereus with a bloody feast cooked with his son's entrails. Pelues subdues Thetis and though he 'marries' her, the act is quite evident. But since she is a goddess, the narrative presents their union as favourable for the birth of Achilles. Women who rape become horrible mutants as in the case of Salmacis and Hermaphroditus. Aphrodite is also implied to have raped Adonis. But since she is a goddess, the act is ignored and treated as a warning for disobedience. There is another tale of Ixion who was purified by Zeus. But Ixion tried to rape Hera and for that, Zeus sent him down to Tartaros. There he was tied onto a wheel that kept spinning forever.

Myrrha's incest for her father and Phaedra's for her stepson Hippolytus are perfect examples of incest in Greek mythology. Myrrha's lust for Cinyras is a tale of pure incest while Hippolytus is cursed by Aphrodite and becomes a victim. In either case, incest is considered dishonourable and the perpetrators end up dying disgracefully. However, it is an entirely different story with the gods. Zeus married his sister Hera, Cronos married his sister Rhea and Persephone was a child born to Zeus and another of his sister Ceres. Persephone is Hades' niece. Incest can be the result of the ancient custom of marrying within a family to preserve the purity of the lineage. Egyptian pharaohs practised it to maintain the hierarchy within one family.

6. Pre-Iliadic heroes

Achilles and Odysseus are considered 'modern' heroes in Greek mythology. The adventures of Perseus, Hercules, Jason, Meleager and Bellerophon precede them. Ovid's *Metamorphosis* and Apollodorus' *Bibliotheque* list the adventures of these heroes much before Achilles and Odysseus. Again there are many versions of these stories as in the case of the *Iliad*. Perseus is known today for his slaying of the Gorgon Medusa. He did not fly on the Pegasus as the media has us believing. Bellerophon was the one who flew on the Pegasus and killed the Chimaera. Jason obtained the Golden Fleece with the help of Medea. Meleager organised the Calydonian Boar hunt in which Atalanta won. Though these narratives are not as vast or as structured as the *Iliad* and the *Odyssey*, the quest theme originates here. Homer takes up the same structure. But both the *Iliad* and the *Odyssey* remain fragmentary and incomplete. The former ends with the death of Hector and the latter with Odysseus killing off Penelope's suitors. Virgil's *Aeneid* shows the death of Achilles and Apollodorus' *Bibliotheque* shows Odysseus unknowingly killed by Telegonos (his son born to Circe). The epic also shows Telegonos marrying Penelope and Telemachus (Odysseus' son born to Penelope) marrying Circe: "When Telegonos discovered his identity, he lamented bitterly, and took his corpse, and Penelope too, to the land of Circe, where he married Penelope, and Circe sent the pair of them to the Isles of the Blessed" (277).

Achilles is drawn from the physical prowess of Hercules. Likewise, the personality of Odysseus can be matched with Theseus. While the former depends upon his strength, the latter depends on his intelligence. Jason's construction of the Argonaut is quite similar to the Greeks sailing on ships to Troy. Raiding cities, pillaging temples, getting cursed by divine beings, fighting for glory, seducing women, tragic deaths and sacrifices seem to be the themes repeated in all of these heroic narratives. Some of these heroes - Hercules, Achilles, Odysseus - became gods after their deaths and they had their cults in Greece.

7. Murder and ritual purification

The *Oresteia* trilogy of Aeschylus depicts Orestes haunted by the Furies for killing his mother. Orestes had killed Clytemnestra in vengeance for his father. Clytemnestra had plotted with her lover Aegisthus to kill her husband Agamemnon who returned from the Trojan War. Though what Orestes has done is justifiable, he cannot rule Mycenae because he has shed the blood of his family. Such people were doomed to be haunted by the Furies wherever they went. Hercules faces the same fate when he kills his wife Megara. It is not his fault as he was driven mad by Hera. Perseus could not rule Argos because he had killed his grandfather.

Ritual purifications could spare the hero from the fate of the Furies. Athena purifies Orestes after a trial. Hercules is purified by many kings. He performs the twelve labours to please King Eurystheus. He is also sold into slavery and serves Queen Omphale to get her purification. Meleager kills his uncles over a brawl and he faces the same fate though he dies before receiving any purification. Sometimes the perpetrator served kings or oracles for a certain time. This service was considered purification. The architect Daedalus served Minos for killing his nephew Talos. This purification was either a quest or a service that supposedly transformed the hero's hubris. The hero could move on with his life only after the purification.

8. Apples in Greek mythology

Apples were symbols of fertility and beauty in Greek mythology. It was customary to throw apples at the bride and the groom on their wedding day to ensure fertility. That was why Eris threw the apple of discord at the wedding of Peleus and Thetis. Hera had an orchard of golden apples. These were gifted to her at her wedding by Gaia, goddess of Earth. The Hesperides or the daughters of Atlas, beautiful nymphs, were charged with the duty of protecting the orchard. There was also a dragon that protected the apples. Hercules was tasked with getting some of these apples for his eleventh labour.

Since Hera was a goddess of marriage, fertility and wealth, the apples in her garden reflected these qualities. These apples were often a quest treasure prized by heroes and obtained by them at great risk. In Norse mythology, Idunn, the goddess of youth, has a box of golden apples. The other gods and goddesses eat these apples to retain their youth. Apples signified physical beauty, youth and fertility in Western myths. The goddess Aphrodite offered three golden apples to Hippomenes from her garden. Hippomenes threw the apples to distract the swift-footed Atalanta. The apples united them in marriage.

9. The legendary Troy and the Abduction of women

Herodotus records the origins of the conflict between Greeks and Asians because of a series of abductions of women. Book 1 of *The Histories* states that the Phoenicians sailed to Argos to trade their cargo. Several Argive women came down to see the cargo and the king's daughter Io was among them. The Phoenicians abducted the women, including Io, and sailed for Egypt. The Greeks sailed to Colchis and abducted Medea, the princess of Colchis to avenge Io. When the Colchian king sent a messenger to Greece asking for compensation, the Greeks replied that they did not get any for Io. Furthermore, Herodotus asserts that Alexandros (Paris) "heard the stories and wanted to abduct a wife from Hellas for himself, quite confident that he would pay no penalty since the other had not paid either. And so he abducted Helen" (4). The Persians were allies of the Trojans and were angry with the Greeks for creating a fuss over Helen and destroying Troy.

From all this, one can easily understand that the abduction of Helen and the other women was a political move. These abductions were quite common and the women were compliant with them. The Persians believed that it was not dignified for the Greeks to declare war over a woman. The abducted women were either sold off as slaves or taken as concubines by kings. So was the case of women taken as booty after a war. Apollodorus writes that Hecuba was given to Odysseus as spoils of war after the Trojan War. Neoptolemus, the son of Achilles, got Andromache and had a son by her. His name was Molossos. Women were essential goods, sorted out and taken according to their beauty, social hierarchy and wealth. Rich kings like Agamemnon got the best pick. These women accepted their fates and submitted without a fight.

It is not surprising to read that Troy was attacked many times by the Greeks. Hercules was the first to breach the wall of Troy with just eighteen ships. Paris' abduction of Helen was not the first either. Theseus and his friend Perithous vowed to marry the daughters of Zeus. Theseus abducted and raped Helen when she was just twelve years old. He left her at his castle in Athens and went on to help his friend. Perithous went a step further and tried to abduct Persephone. Hades got angry and tricked them both. They were made to sit on the Chair of Forgetfulness. Perithous stuck to it forever while Theseus was rescued by Hercules. In the absence of Theseus, Helen's brothers Castor and Pollux rescued her. Most of the time, the abduction of these women either led to war or was used as a pretext to start a war. Many of these women were daughters of Zeus, Poseidon or some other minor divinity. In that case, possessing them was considered a privilege much like bringing back an expensive souvenir from your vacation.

10. Sacrifices and libations

Prometheus was the one who showed humans how to sacrifice to the gods. Homer describes the ritual sacrifice quite elaborately in the *Iliad* and the *Odyssey*. Kings sacrificed before going to war, on special occasions and for fertility. The sacrificial victims were bulls, heifers, cows, boars, rams and ewes. Sometimes, human sacrifice was also given. Agamemnon sacrificed his youngest daughter

Iphigeneia on the altar of Artemis to ensure victory in the Trojan War. Polyxena, the youngest daughter of Priam and Hecuba, was sacrificed on the tomb of Achilles to protect the Greeks from storms on the voyage home. Achilles sacrificed many beasts and Trojan victims on the day of Patroclus' funeral just because he wanted to.

In the case of animals, the victim was doused with wine. The king or the one giving the sacrifice slit the throat of the victim and bled it to death. Then the victim was cut up and roasted on a spit. The best portions, especially the thigh fat rolled around the bones, were offered to the gods first. The remaining portions were cut down for the feast that ensued. The gods took these seriously and were offended if things went wrong. Poseidon was furious when Minos did not give his best bull in sacrifice as he had promised. Zeus was angry when Lycaon tested him with human meat.

Libations were food and drink offerings given before every meal. A portion of the cooked meal was always offered to Hestia, goddess of the household before eating. The wine was poured on the ground before drinking. Menelaus was offering libations on the feast to celebrate the peace between Greece and Troy. It was customary for hosts to give libations before feeding their guests. Libation bowls made of gold and silver were given as gifts between warriors and kings.

Bibliography

Herodotus. *The Histories*. Translated by Robert B. Strassler, Anchor Books, 2009.

Apollodorus. *The Library of Greek Mythology*. Translated by Robin Hard, OxfordUniversity Press, 1997.

Tales of Yore

THE LAUREL TREE

"Apollo walked as in a tower of flames.
As Phoebus burned with love young Daphne fled
As though she feared love's name. . ."Ovid,
Metamorphoses Book I [17]

Zeus, the mighty thunderer sat on his golden throne in Mt. Olympus as he watched over the new world. All the other gods and goddesses took their places around him in the great throne hall. Zeus had destroyed the world! Everyone waited for his next move. The Deluge[1] swallowed everything dark and evil. Deucalion and Pyrrha[2] gave birth to new life, emerging purer from the storm. The god of Olympus was pleased. But even among the new light, darkness found a way. Python, the demon of destruction, roamed free and left death in his wake. Bright and far-shooting Apollo took upon himself the task of slaying the abominable serpent. He aimed at the heavens and killed the demon with his shower of golden arrows. To celebrate the great victory, young men all over Greece brought oak garlands to the Golden One's shrine. The Pythian Games were held at his sacred shrine of Delphi[3] to honour the victory.

The victory brought fame and with it, pride and then jealousy. Apollo taunted Cupid and said that the bow and arrows were his (Apollo's) sacred weapons that slew enormous beasts like Python. Such mighty tools were not meant for something as weak and playful as love. Cupid got angry and shot a golden arrow at Apollo when he was looking at a beautiful maiden. To teach Apollo a lesson, he shot the maiden with a lead arrow. The golden arrow was the arrow of passionate love that burned Apollo's heart in desire. The lead arrow made the maiden hate Apollo. Now in those days of yore, it was not uncommon for divine beings to fall in love with mortal men or women. These beings even had children with mortal humans and this caused much transformation of life forms on the Earth.

The beautiful maiden whose heart bore the lead arrow was Daphne, the elusive daughter of the River King Peneus. She rejected all the suitors her father brought before her. She hoped to remain an eternal virgin like Artemis. Her heart became heavy with hatred and depression. Apollo saw her at the river bank and approached her with words of love. She ran away in disgust and hatred. Apollo saw her beautiful hair flying behind her; her clothes torn by rocks and her breath panting. He chased her over hills and valleys, across crystal rivers, dales and orchards. He saw himself possessing her and yet, this was the first time his prophecy failed. Daphne was swift of foot but mortal still. He called out to her that he was Apollo, the Golden One, slayer of Python. But she did not listen.

Daphne grew tired and finally slowed down a bit. Apollo gained on her and when she saw that defeat was near, she prayed aloud to her father. She requested the river to cover her with green earth. As soon as she said this, a drowsiness crept in and she stood heavy. She couldn't move her limbs. Her ivory skin became the tough bark of a tree. Her hands and hair transformed into long leafy branches. Her beautiful face was framed with green leaves. When Apollo reached her, he could still hear her heart beating its last. Daphne became the laurel, the symbol of poetry and wisdom. Apollo took the laurel as his sacred seal, his symbol and crowned his golden hair with her leaves. Roman soldiers wear the laurel as a symbol of victory when they return home from battles. Poets and victors are crowned with laurels on the day of the Pythian Games. Apollo could never forget his first love and carried her in his hair wherever he went.

CHAPTER THREE

The Peacock's Feathers

"The frightful Argos whose unnatural head
Shone with a hundred eyes, a perfect jailer
For man or beast:"Ovid, *Metamorphoses* Book I [25]

The River King Inachus had a beautiful daughter named Io. Her beauty surpassed all the other princesses of Greece. Zeus, the All-Seeing One, had her in his eyes for a long time. Zeus was married to Hera, the goddess of wealth. She was also his sister. Many of these mythical tales show divine beings marrying their own siblings. It is common in both Greek and Egyptian myths. Anyway, to make matters short, Hera was an extremely jealous goddess. She grew green with envy when she saw her husband with Io. Zeus knew this and changed poor Io into a white cow. Hera was not without her wiles. She took the cow as a gift Zeus could not refuse.

Once she had the cow in her possession, Hera was still anxious. So she sent her demon half-brother Argos to keep watch over Io (the cow). Zeus could not secretly visit her anymore. Not with Argos watching her with his innumerable eyes. Now, to talk about Argos; he was a demonic being with a thousand eyes all over his body (or what looked like a body anyway). He was always awake because his eyes took turns at watching the cow. When some of the eyes closed to sleep, others remained awake. Zeus was at a loss. He sent Hermes to rescue the girl and subdue the demon.

Hermes was a trickster, a messenger and the god who stole Apollo's lyre. He already had a trick up his sleeve when he reached Argos. Hermes played on his pipes for Argos who had never heard such sweet music. The prudent god told Argos the tale of Pan and his pipes to make him sleep. Pan had fallen in love with Syrinx, a flower spirit in the mountains of Arcady. But she had run away from him and begged the fountain nymphs to change her. Pan caught up to her but all he could grab were a set of reeds. He blew through them and made such sweet music.

From that day on, he had kept the pipes as his sacred symbol. Hermes' tale and music made Argos fall asleep. When the demon's eyes drooped, Hermes quickly slew him and rescued Io. Hera was furious and wailed when she saw her half-brother dead. With the skill of an expert jeweller, she took Argos' dead eyes and placed them on the feathers of a peacock. From that day onwards, the peacock became Hera's sacred bird. So, now you know why the peacock has such colourful eyes!

And what happened to Io? Just like many of the mortal victims, Io wandered as a cow all alone till she reached the banks of the river Nile. She took a quick drink from the cool water and lo! She was magically transformed back into a maiden. More than that, she became an immortal being, the goddess Isis. Aset was her Egyptian name and she was worshipped along with her husband Osiris (Egyptian: Asar) and son Horus (Greek: Epaphus) in Upper and Lower Egypt. There she was honoured as the Lady of the Throne, the Lady of Ornaments and the Queen of Upper and Lower Egypt.

CHAPTER FOUR

THE RAVEN

"'I told Minerva (Athena) what the girls had done,
And I, who was still then her favourite bird,
Was sent among the black birds of the night!'" Ovid,
Metamorphoses Book II [48]

The Raven was once Athena's sacred bird before the Owl succeeded her. This magnificent black bird had been a princess named Coronis, the daughter of Coroneus of Phocis. Poseidon was inflamed with her beauty and she called to Artemis for help from her pursuer. The goddess of the hunt changed her into a gentle white raven and she flew way out of Poseidon's grasp. Coronis was Athena's companion for a long time. But Coronis was always jealous of the wise and powerful goddess.

One dark and windy day, Athena gave a box to three trusted friends of hers and asked them to keep it secret. They were never supposed to open the box. The three friends - Pendrosos, Herse and Aglauros - could not contain their curiosity. They opened the box and stood aghast at the horrible sight within. Inside the box lay Erichthonius[4], the half-human half-demon son of Athena, who was worshipped as a virgin goddess of war. "Virgin" in those days had a different meaning from that of the modern usage. The classical "virgin" was an independent, strong and self-reliant woman. Anyway, the white raven Coronis beamed with happiness. She could use this to dishonour Athena. Coronis spread the birth of the infamous monster far and wide. Athena was angry. The warrior-goddess caught the raven and made it black. Coronis lost her job. Athena took Nyctimene[5], the Owl, as her sacred bird. Athena nurtured Erichthonius till he grew up to become one of the legendary rulers of Athens.

CHAPTER FIVE

The Healer Who Gave Life to the Dead

"'Take notice of the serpent on my wand
Who coils it round, and you must know him well,
For he shall be myself tomorrow morning,
Larger than life as heavenly beings are.'" Ovid,
Metamorphoses Book XV [429]

Apollo's lovers always had tragic fates. So it was with Coronis (not Athena's sidekick mentioned before). She was pregnant with Apollo's child but she was with another mortal, Ischys. When the god found out, he became pale and the laurels melted from his curls. In a fit of fury, he took aim and shot his mortal arrow at her heart. He lost his child for which he wept piteously. Being the god of healing, he tried to breathe life into her. It was futile. Then he felt the child's strong heart still beating within his dead mother's womb. In a flash, Apollo pulled out his golden dagger and tore Coronis' womb. He took the child to the cave of Master Chiron[6], the Centaur.

Chiron's daughter, red-haired Ocyrhoe prophesied that the child would become the greatest healer the Earth has ever known. He will even breathe life into the dead. For which, Zeus will strike him. Then he will be reborn again as a god. Apollo named him Aesculapius and taught him all about medicine. Chiron taught him how to defend himself. Once when he was in a cave, a snake crawled up on his staff and taught him the secret art of necromancy. With this, he brought back dead kings, princes and heroes back to life.

Hades, the King of the Underworld and Master of the Dead complained to his brother Zeus that the Underworld was becoming empty. Aesculapius was upsetting the delicate balance of life and death. As Ocyrhoe prophesied, Zeus struck the healer with his thunderbolt. Later, Aesculapius was reincarnated as a god and taken to Mt. Olympus upon Apollo's request. The original Hippocratic Oath (taken by doctors upon completing their course) began with an invocation to Apollo and Aesculapius. Even today, pharmacies and chemists have adopted the symbol of Aesculapius' staff. He is also identified with the Egyptian deity Imhotep.

Note: The Staff of Aesculapius and the Caduceus are almost similar and often used wrong in place of the other. The Staff of Aesculapius is a rod with a single serpent coiled onto it. The Caduceus is a winged rod with two serpents coiled around glancing at each other. The Caduceus is the sacred symbol of Hermes representing his powers as a messenger god.

CHAPTER SIX

ECHO AND NARCISSUS

"'O may he love himself alone,' he cried,
'And yet fail in that great love.' The curse was heard
By wakeful Nemesis." Ovid, *Metamorphoses* Book III
[72]

The City of Boeotia was built upon the spot where Zeus fell in love with Europa[7]. Tiresias[8] became the legendary Seer of Boeotia. One day, a nymph came to him to ask about her son Narcissus. Tiresias prophesied that the boy would live as long "as he knew himself." Narcissus grew up to be an exceptionally handsome youth when he was only sixteen. Many young maidens and nymphs came to stare at him. One among them, Echo fell so madly in love with him. Echo was a cursed nymph. She could not speak unless spoken to. Even then, she could only repeat what the other person spoke. She had no voice of her own. She had hidden away the nymphs cherished by Zeus, so Hera had cursed her. Poor, poor Echo. But fate had something far worse for her.

Narcissus had a favourite spot in the woods by the lake. He heard Echo following him on her soft feet. He called out, "Is anybody here?"

"Here..." came the reply.

"Come," he said. "Come..." he heard.

"Here we shall meet," he said and got back the same answer. Only this time, he saw a beautiful green-haired nymph come out from the trees, water dripping all over her. But he rejected her with harsh words and she faded away in depression until there was nothing left of poor Echo except her haunting voice. Proud Narcissus treated many other lovers with cruel words when one of them raised a prayer to Nemesis, the goddess of vengeance. "O may he love himself alone, And yet fail in that great love," was the prayer which Nemesis granted.

When Narcissus reached his favourite lake, silver-clear, he bent to drink the water. He saw his reflection - he felt himself cut from the finest marble, the stars were his eyes, hair as bright as Apollo's and his ivory limbs. He fell passionately in love with himself. He tried to kiss the reflection but his arms grasped only the cold water. He didn't eat or sleep. He stayed day and night by the lake staring at himself. Echo's voice repeated his sighs and curses. He starved himself and went straight down to Hades' kingdom. His sisters shaved their heads and wailed in sorrow. They built his bier and raised the pyre but his body vanished. They saw a small golden flower with white-rimmed petals on the spot where his body lay. This wonderful flower is called narcissus and too much self-love is called Narcissism. This is a personality disorder in which people have a need for excessive attention, troubled relationships and a lack of empathy for others.

CHAPTER SEVEN

PYRAMUS AND THISBE

"What eyes are sharper than the eyes
Of Love? The lovers found the slit and made it
The hidden mouthpiece of their voices where
Love's subtle words in sweetest whispers came. . ."Ovid,
Metamorphoses Book IV [89]

The beautiful land of Babylon was ruled by the iron-willed Queen Semiramis[9]. Pyramus and Thisbe were children of Babylonian nobles. They were neighbours and grew up together. But when they fell in love, their parents came between them and constructed a huge wall through their homes. They found a tiny fissure in the wall between them and used it to whisper to each other. After all, what eyes are sharper than those of love?

They met every evening and complained about their sad fate. But there was not a kind soul to take pity on them. One day, they came to a decision. They would meet that night on the site of Ninus'[10] tomb under the shadow of a famous mulberry tree by the river. (Note that the lovers choose the tomb of the legendary hero who fell in love with the warrior-queen Semiramis)Then they would elope. The day seemed too long and the Sun lagged on his journey. As soon as darkness fell, Thisbe, veiled and unseen, slipped out silently among the shadows. She ran to the tomb and took her place beneath the tree. She dreamed of being married to her love forever. But alas! A lioness approached her stealthily from behind the tree. The beast's jaws were blood-lined for she had fed recently. Thisbe ran and hid in a cave, leaving her veil behind. The lioness came down to the river, drank her fill and sniffed at the veil. Then she tore it off and left.

A moment later, Pyramus arrived. He saw the footprints of the lioness and the shredded blood-stained veil of Thisbe. He put two and two together and wailed for the lost Thisbe. Then he decided, "One night shall be the killing of two lovers." He blamed himself for sending an unarmed maiden into the forest at night. Now Thisbe was dead because of him. He took the veil to the tree, kissed it and covered it with his tears. "Now drink my blood," he said as he thrust his sword into his side. As he pulled out his sword, blood streamed from him and sprayed across the fruits of the tree. The mulberry's milk-white fruits became red. They have been red ever since.

Poor Thisbe came down from the cave looking for Pyramus. Perhaps he was late? Or had he left her? Had he betrayed her? She trembled. She saw the mulberry fruits and wondered if they were red in the first place. Then she saw her wounded lover fighting for life. She tore her hair and wailed in grief. As she wept, his eyes rolled toward her and closed forever. "By your own hand, even your love has killed you," she said. "Only Lord Hades has the power to separate us now. Let our parents see us and understand that we will be together in our tomb. Oh, tree! You shall bear witness to two deaths now. May your dark fruit bear the colour of mourning!" said she. Then she took the bloody sword and stabbed her beating heart. The fruits of the tree turned pink.

CHAPTER EIGHT

THE SUNFLOWER AND THE FRANKINCENSE

"Of the pale violet; a flower came
Where once herself had been, now fast in earth,
Though less than human, yet her love unchanged,
She turned her face always to meet the sun." Ovid,
Metamorphoses Book IV [95-6]

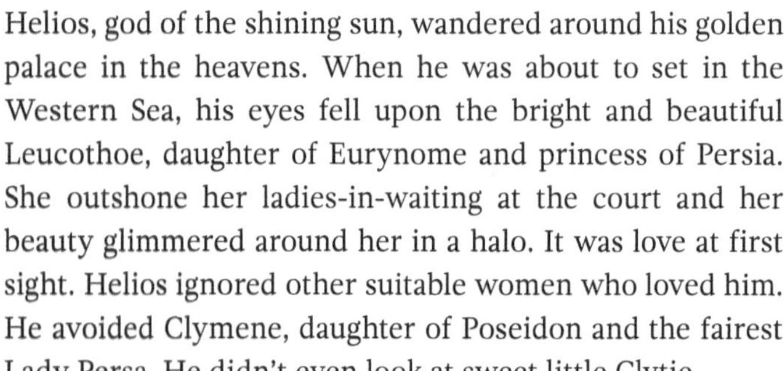

Helios, god of the shining sun, wandered around his golden palace in the heavens. When he was about to set in the Western Sea, his eyes fell upon the bright and beautiful Leucothoe, daughter of Eurynome and princess of Persia. She outshone her ladies-in-waiting at the court and her beauty glimmered around her in a halo. It was love at first sight. Helios ignored other suitable women who loved him. He avoided Clymene, daughter of Poseidon and the fairest Lady Persa. He didn't even look at sweet little Clytie.

The flaming horses of Helios grazed under the Western axis. They ate ambrosia instead of grass. When Nyx, the goddess of Night, darkened the horizon, Helios entered Leucothoe's chamber in the guise of her mother. Leucothoe was in the midst of twelve maidens, spinning. He took the spindle from her white hand and commanded all the others to leave. Then he revealed his true self. "I am the one who makes all the seasons of the year, each day, each hour and who looks at you with delight!" he said and shone in his splendour. Leucothoe dropped her spindle in terror. But she could not resist and welcomed the sun's embrace.

Clytie saw Helios with Leucothoe and went green with envy. She quickly spread the news to everyone in the city, including Leucothoe's father. He was ruthless and cold. He refused to listen to her pleas. With brute anger, he tossed her into a pit and buried her alive. Helios tried to open the pit with his rays but it was too late. She had already descended to the dark realm of Hades. He poured sweet nectar over her grave and said, "one day your spirit shall be felt in heaven." Her body melted and fragrance filled the air. A tiny shoot of frankincense broke through the tomb. Ever since Leucothoe's spirit has lifted sacred spaces in perfume.

Clytie felt that Helios would come to her now that Leucothoe was dead. But she was promptly rejected. He hated her even more because she was the reason for his beloved's death. She became dejected and pale. Soon she became insane and wandered the field naked. Her face turned only to look at Helios' passage in the sky. Her limbs rooted to the earth, her colour became green and her head a beautiful strange brown surrounded by flaming petals. She became the sunflower and her love remains unchanged as she turns her face to greet the sun.

CHAPTER NINE

PERSEUS AND MEDUSA

"And Perseus carried as a proof of valour
A memorable prize - all that was left
Of a wild snake-haired creature, fought and won -"
Ovid, *Metamorphoses* Book IV [106]

King Acrisius ruled over the land of Argos, known far and wide for his wealth and power. He denied the existence of Bacchus as a god and forbade his people to observe the god's festivities. The Oracle of Delphi prophesied that Acrisius would be dethroned and destroyed by his grandson. So he locked up his daughter in a bronze tower and forbade her to have any relationships. He was cursed and soon enough his daughter, Princess Danaë bore a baby boy, the son of Zeus. The god had visited the princess in a shower of gold falling into the bronze tower. Danaë named the boy 'Perseus' which meant "destroyer of cities". She hoped the boy would bring an end to her father's tyranny.

Things didn't go well for the princess and the boy. Acrisius was furious as he hated Zeus and his daughter. The sight of Perseus gave him shivers down his spine. He placed the child and the mother in a wooden coffin and threw it into the sea cursing Zeus and his offspring. Danaë's prayer was heard by Zeus and the coffin washed ashore on the island of Seriphos. They were taken in by fisherman Dictys, brother of King Polydictes, ruler of Seriphos. Dictys took care of Perseus as his own.

Time passed and Perseus grew up into a handsome young warrior. He was good at both the fishing net and the sword. King Polydictes had an eye on Danaë and wanted her as his wife. But Perseus knew that Polydictes was a war-mongering tyrant. One day, Polydictes arranged for a huge banquet in his hall. He declared that he was going to ask for the hand of Hippodamia, daughter of King Oenomaos. There was a prophecy that Oenomaos would be slain by his son-in-law. So the king fixed a chariot race for all the suitors of his daughter. They would have to race the king himself and if they failed, Oenomaos would kill them. He had already killed eighteen princes in the race. Polydictes called for the best horses from his men to participate in the race. He saw Perseus walk into the hall and called him, "Perseus, my fine lad! What horse have you brought for your king?"

"I'm sorry, my liege, but I don't have any horse to offer. You know I'm poor," said Perseus. "But I can offer you anything else you ask, sire," he added. Now, that was a mistake. Polydictes was a cunning man and he was expecting this naivete from Perseus.

"Honour what you've said, my lad. Take an oath in the name of Styx," said Polydictes. Perseus swore an oath in the name of the River Styx. Anything sworn in the name of the rivers of the Underworld, especially Styx, must be kept on life or death. It was a sacred law of Greece and Rome.

"Bring me the head of the Gorgon Medusa, boy!" claimed Polydictes and Perseus could not refuse. Medusa was one of three Gorgons, female monsters who had snakes for hair and their gaze turned any living being to stone. Among the three, Stheno and Euryale were immortal. Medusa was the only mortal Gorgon. This was because Medusa was raped by Poseidon inside Athena's temple. Athena had changed Medusa's beautiful hair into snakes to protect her. Killing her was a big deal and Perseus knew he was going to need all the help he could get. He prayed to Athena, the blue-eyed goddess of wisdom and war, and she appeared. She asked him to go to the Graeae, sisters of the Gorgons. They would disclose the whereabouts of the Hesperides who would give him magical weapons to kill Medusa.

The Graeae were three old witches named Deino, Enyo and Pemphredo, daughters of the Titan Phorcys[11]; horrible hags who shared one eye and tooth between them. They had the gift of prophecy and sorcery. Perseus approached their dark cave and called out to them.

"Greetings, Oh Graeae, wise women of the past! Tell me where I will find the Hesperides," he said.

"Oh, it's Perseus...noble son of Zeus! We know why you're here. We know that you're after Medusa's head. Why should we betray our sister for you?" they whined and growled like animals. Perseus lurched forward and grabbed their eye, the one that they shared and the one capable of looking into the future.

"No! Not the eye! Give us the eye, boy! And we will tell you everything!" they yelled. They told him that the Hesperides lived on Mt. Atlas on the North African coast. Then Perseus returned their eye and left on his journey to the far coast of Africa. The Hesperides were seven daughters of the Titan Atlas. They were golden nymphs of the evening chosen by Hera to guard her sacred orchard located in the West. They protected the golden apples of youth, the fruits of Hera. It was from this garden that Eris pulled up the apple of strife, the very fruit that caused the Trojan War.

The Hesperides told Perseus that Medusa lived on the outskirts of the Underworld. They gave him a gift: a kibisis or a magic sack to bind Medusa's head. Zeus appeared and gifted Perseus a harpe, a sickle-sword made of adamantine steel that cut through anything. Hermes offered him his very own winged sandals. Hades offered his Helm of Darkness capable of making the wearer invisible. Last of all, Athena presented her Aegis, or magical shield that would protect him from any danger. Armed with the divine gifts and the blessings of the gods, Perseus entered Medusa's cave. He saw her coming from a distance and used Athena's Aegis to see Medusa's reflection. That way, he did not have to look at her directly. He chopped off her head in one swift stroke with the harpe and wrapped it up in the kibisis. Pegasus and Chrysador were born from Medusa's blood. Pegasus was a black winged horse and Chrysador was a young man with a golden sword. These two monsters pursued Perseus but he put on Hades' Helm of Darkness and they couldn't see him. Perseus returned to Argos but had other adventures on the way. But that is a story for another day.

CHAPTER TEN

ANDROMEDA AND CETUS

"So Perseus dove upon the raging dragon,
Thrusting, hilt-deep, the sword into its shoulder.
Burning with its gaped wound, the dragon reared
Its bulk in air, then dived, veered like a boar. . ." Ovid,
Metamorphoses Book IV [110]

Perseus slew Medusa and took her head. He flew on Hermes' sandals and stopped in Ethiopia on the way to Seriphos. He was already a hero and hosted in the court of King Cepheus and Queen Cassiopeia. The proud queen boasted that her only daughter Andromeda was the most beautiful creature in the world. She went so far to say that Andromeda was even more beautiful than the Nereids, the nymphs of the sea. These Nereids were the fifty daughters of Nereus and Doris. They accompanied Poseidon and wore red coral crowns on their hair. They sang melodiously and often guided sailors. Anyway, Poseidon was angry and sent Cetus, a huge sea monster that ravaged Ethiopia.

Cepheus and Cassiopeia were horrified. The king's men attacked Cetus but it could not be slain by any mortal. The Oracle of Ammon in Egypt claimed that the princess must be sacrificed to the beast to appease Poseidon. There was no other way. Andromeda was stripped and tied naked to a rock that faced the sea. Perseus saw the monster approaching, its jaw wide open and its tail lashing behind. He climbed to the rock, took out Medusa's head from his kibisis and held it to the monster's view. There was nothing but a huge rumbling sound as the monster became stone and crashed into the sea. Andromeda was saved and Perseus asked King Cepheus for her hand in marriage. Cepheus was glad and there was a grand wedding feast.

But there was a problem. There is one in all good tales. Andromeda had already been engaged to the tyrant Phineus. Now Phineus was only interested in expanding his territory and gaining the wealth of Ethiopia through Andromeda. He marched into the wedding feast with his soldiers, all armed to the teeth. He walked straight to Perseus and told him that he had come to claim his lost bride and face the avenger. Perseus said nothing. He simply opened his kibisis and turned Phineus and his men to stone. When he returned to Seriphos, King Polydictes was not only furious, but also jealous. He still claimed Danaë as his wife. Perseus turned the tyrant to stone with Medusa's head. Then he married his mother to Dictes, the fisherman and next king of Seriphos.

Things were not peaceful for Perseus. He learned of his birth and went back to Argos. Acrisius received the hero in hatred and declared that Perseus was a liar. "This man here is a traitor and a liar. He is capable of deceiving the innocent just like Zeus!" he yelled.

"I have slain the Gorgon. It's true," Perseus said.

"Then let me see her head," Acrisius claimed.

"Choose your words carefully, king. For you do not know what comes next," Perseus warned.

"Then it's a lie. I knew it. You're just like your mother," Acrisius remarked. This infuriated Perseus. He opened the kibisis and brought out the Gorgon's head. Acrisius became a statue of stone, his grimace frozen in his lips. Thus the prophecy was fulfilled and Acrisius was dethroned by his grandson.

But Greek law stated that a person who murdered another, even to defend himself, must be exiled. The murderer cannot return unless he had been purified by divine presence. So Perseus gave Argos to Megapenthes and got back Tiryns in exchange. Megapenthes was his cousin and ruler of Tiryns. Little did he know that Megapenthes was going to kill him to avenge his uncle. Perseus and Andromeda ruled Tiryns and founded Mycenae, the land later ruled by Agamemnon during the Trojan War. Perseus returned the divine gifts to their owners. He offered Medusa's head as a gift to Athena. The goddess placed the head on her Aegis and wears it to this day. Perseus and Andromeda had a long and peaceful reign. Their son Perses was the founder of the Persian empire. The great Hercules himself was a descendant of Perseus.

CHAPTER ELEVEN

PERSEPHONE AND THE POMEGRANATE

"And as she strolled there, plucked a dark pomegranate,
Unwrapped its yellow skin, and swallowed seven
Of its blood-purpled seeds." Ovid, *Metamorphoses* Book
V [134]

Aphrodite, the gleaming goddess of beauty looked at the world from her mountain temple in Eryx. She saw many mortals and immortals feeling the pain of love. Love conquered all and lived even in the darkest depths of the sea. However, the goddess shook her golden tresses when she saw the dark realms of Hades. This was not to be. She called her young son, Cupid, the god of love and told him, "Look here, my son, why have you spared the lands of Tartaros[12] alone? Why not increase our empire of love? You know that Artemis and Athena are arraigned against me. Now Ceres' daughter, young Persephone wants to join the cult of Artemis too. Let's connect her fate to the dark realms." Cupid unlocked his quiver and searched for the best arrow. There were some lead arrows of hatred and golden ones that brought love. He chose the sharpest of all the golden arrows and shot it into Hades' heart when he was looking at Persephone.

The town of Henna was famous for its lakes and rivers. It was such a fertile land because it was blessed by the presence of Ceres, the goddess of farming, vegetation and abundance. Lake Pergus was the best lake in all of Henna. It was surrounded with beautiful lilies and violets hanging beautifully over the water. Swans played with green-haired nymphs who sang melodiously. Persephone, the young and beautiful daughter of Ceres, played by the lake every day. She plucked the flowers and made a wreath for her pretty head. Her friends decked her flowing red hair with violets. She did not notice Hades staring at her with Cupid's flames in his heart.

Hades snatched the girl and vanished in his chariot. Persephone called in terror to her friends but they were afraid of death. She prayed to her mother while Hades spurred his horses and flew faster than the wind. They flew through canyons and waterfalls before reaching the stream of Arethusa[13]. Cynane, a nymph and friend of Ceres' lived here. Cyane recognised Persephone's voice and raised the waters up like a barrier. "Sir, you shall not pass. You are not the rightful son-in-law of Ceres," she said. Hades raised his pitchfork and struck through the water barrier. He sped down to deepest Tartaros and Cyane knew that Persephone was now lost forever. Just before diving back, she saw Persephone's girdle floating on the water. She kept it so she could guide Ceres.

Now all this time, Ceres was searching for her daughter. She asked Aurora of the dawn and Hesperus of the evening stars but none had seen Persephone. Ceres lit two torches from the fire of the volcano Aetna and wandered till dawn. She travelled across the seas and climbed mountains. Finally, she reached Cyane's stream. Cyane tossed the girdle across and Ceres knew it was her daughter's. She smashed the ploughs and killed all the crops. She murdered the seedlings and destroyed the harvest. People started dying of starvation. It was then that Arethusa, nymph of the stream where Cyane lived rose and spoke to Ceres, "O mother of vegetation, goddess of abundance, forgive this land that worships you. You know I travel through many lands. Lately, I meandered through Styx of the Underworld and it was there that I saw your daughter. She is not the queen of the Underworld. Though she is sad, she is the wife of Hades now."

When the mother heard the news, she stood as if she was turned to stone. She stepped on her chariot and flew to Mt. Olympus. She went straight to the throne of Zeus, her hair wild and her face flushed. She spoke thus, "Hail, all-father and most powerful sovereign of the universe! I come to speak, to plead the case of my child. Persephone was abducted by your brother Hades. It seems he has married her. She does not deserve a thief for her husband."

"She is my daughter but I must not be partial here. Hades has truly married her out of love. It's not a disgrace to marry my own brother," said Zeus.

"But my lord, Hades of all men! He rules over the dead! His realms are dark and his castle horrible! Persephone cannot live there," Ceres pleaded.

"He needs your goodwill. He does not rule the heavens, indeed. But he is a powerful ruler nonetheless. If your will is fixed on her divorce, then you shall get her back on one condition. If she has not eaten anything from the Underworld, she may return to you," Zeus concluded. Ceres went back to the earth. Zeus sent Hermes the messenger to fetch the girl from the Underworld.

Meanwhile, Persephone wandered into the gardens of the Underworld. She saw nothing but black flowers and ferns full of ash. The grass had dried up and hurt her feet. There was darkness everywhere she looked. But Hades was kind to her. She was extremely hungry as she had not eaten anything for days. Hades plucked a pomegranate and gave it to her. Poor Persephone ate seven of its blood-red seeds. That sealed her fate forever. Hermes saw this and reported it to Zeus. The thunderer alighted upon the Earth and announced to Ceres that Persephone was to live with Hades as queen of the Underworld for six months. She could live with her mother for another six. Hence, it is summer when she is with her mother and cold winter when leaves for the Underworld.

ARACHNE, THE SPIDER

"Not even Pallas nor blue-fevered Envy
Could damn Arachne's work. The gold-haired goddess
Raged at the girl's success, struck through her loom,
Tore down the scenes of wayward joys in Heaven. . ."
Ovid, *Metamorphoses* Book VI [144]

In the city of Maeonia, there lived a poor young girl named Arachne. She was the daughter of the craftsman Idmon of Colophon. Though Arachne was neither beautiful nor wealthy, she was famous for her craft. She was known all over Lydia as a master weaver, a maker of beautiful tapestries that adorned the halls of many kings. Idmon procured rare silks dyed in purple and scarlet for her fine hands and she made a fine living with her craft. The nymphs left their water of Pactolus to see her work. The yarn flew through her shuttle and she created masterpieces that shone like the midday sun. Everyone said that she was blessed by Pallas Athena, the goddess of wisdom, war and the arts. But she denied it in pride. "Why should the gods and goddesses take credit for everything we do? Let Athena compete against me and we shall see," she said haughtily.

Athena appeared in the guise of a crone, leaning on her staff. She said, "My dear girl, remember that the gods and goddesses possess true wisdom. Give your goddess grace for your skill and ask her to forgive you."

"You old fool! You have a feeble mind. Go advise your daughters or daughters-in-law if you have them. I'll advise myself. By the way, where is your goddess? Why is she afraid to rival me?" yelled Arachne. Athena took off her disguise and the crowd fell to their knees. Arachne flushed but did not bow down.

Looms were set across and the competition began. The shuttles flashed through their ardent fingers at lightning speed. Athena wove a tapestry depicting all the gods and goddesses in their glory punishing and transforming evil-doers. Arachne wove the lustful adventures of the gods and their human victims. She presented Zeus in his innumerable forms luring innocent women. The competition came to a close and Arachne's was the best. Not even Athena could beat her. The tapestry seemed to be alive! The gold-haired goddess tore the tapestry in fury, struck Arachne's loom and slashed the girl's face thrice with the shuttle. Arachne could not take such humiliation. What had she done? Wasn't she the winner? She would rather die than suffer humiliation.

Arachne twisted a fine rope around her neck and hanged herself. Athena, with a twist of mercy, lifted her and said, "So shall you live, you proud girl, to swing and to weave forever." And lo! Arachne's body shrivelled. She grew eight legs and became a spider. She jumped across the goddess' palm and went up weaving her thread. So, now you know where the spider comes from. Did you know that spiders are technically called Arachnids?

CHAPTER THIRTEEN

NIOBE AND LATONA

"'There she had twins, while I've had seven times
As much as she. Of course, I'm very happy. I am too
rich in making
Boys and girls, too rich for Fortune to outwit. . .'" Ovid,
Metamorphoses Book VI [147]

Niobe was the proud queen of Tantalis, a beautiful
fertile island in Greece. She and her husband, King
Amphion[14] had fourteen children. Queen Niobe was proud
of her many children but she was more proud that she
was very fertile. Bearing many kids in those days was
considered the best quality of a woman. Grecian queens
would often compete with their rivals to prove they had
fertile wombs! One fine day, Manto the Seeress passed by.
She entered a state of trance and called out to all women,
"O you women of Tantalis, go to the temple of Latona.
Worship the goddess and her twins. And don't forget to
bind your hair with laurel!" The women followed her words
and worshipped the goddess and her twins.

Niobe refused to go to Latona's temple. The tall queen came robed in purple to the streets, handsome as angry women look, and shook her hair. Her long tresses fell about her like a cascade. She shouted out to the women, "Are you all mad? To pray to beings you've never heard of? Why do you worship Latona? My father Tantalus was the only mortal king who ate with the gods. My mother Dione was one of the Pleiades[15]. My grandfather Atlas[16] bears the world on his shoulders. My other grandfather is Zeus himself. My husband Amphion built this city by playing his harp. I am rich, beautiful and respected. But more than that, look at my seven beautiful daughters! Have you ever seen more beautiful beings? Look at my seven strong sons! This places me above Titaness Latona. She was a fugitive. Heaven, nor Earth, nor Sea would welcome her. She gave birth to only two children on this island, a miserable creature. Nothing can outwit me, outrank me. Strip those laurels off your hair and go home!"

The women dropped their wreaths and broke their rituals. Latona saw this and became furious. She spoke to her twins, Apollo and Artemis, "I am your mother. No one but Hera is a greater goddess. Niobe, the proud queen, doubts my powers. Go to her city and destroy it! Show the daughter of Tantalus the true meaning of barrenness!" Phoebus and Phoebe (Apollo and Artemis are called by such names) took their bows, arrows and quivers and alighted on Tantalis. Beneath the castle of Cadmus[17], stood a large training ground. The seven sons of Amphion trained their horses there. Dressed in rich purple, they rode their steeds gallantly. Ismenus cried as an arrow pierced his heart and he fell from his horse. The second son Sipylus fell from an arrow in his neck. Unlucky Phaedimus and Tantalus were killed by the same arrow through their chests, uniting them in death. Alpenor stumbled and bled to death. An arrow flew through Damasichthon's jugular. The last one, Ilionous, fell to his knees in prayer. Apollo granted him a swift death.

When the tragic news reached Niobe, she stood lost in a trance. Amphion thrust his sword into his chest and fell from the throne. Niobe ran to the ground and kissed her dead sons. She raised her eyes to the sky and said, "Drink my tears, Latona! Eat my sorrow! With seven sons I die seven deaths. But still, I have my hope and my victory!" As she said this, she heard the taught music of a bow. Her seven daughters stood around her, dressed in black, mourning their brothers. Six of them fell where they stood and died instantly. Niobe clutched her last child and wept, "O no, not this youngest! Leave her to me! Leave this last one!" But her last child died and fell from her arms.

The childless queen sat, voiceless, faceless and emotionless. The colour faded from her hair, skin and lips. Her eyes stared, glassy and lifeless. Her heart stopped and she became a stone statue. For many centuries, the statue of Niobe continued to weep, mourning the loss of her children.

PHILOMELA, THE NIGHTINGALE

"And as he called a third time, Philomela,
Spotted with blood of Itys, her wild hair
Flying, leaped up to him, tossing the boy's
Blood-dabbled head into his face:" Ovid,
Metamorphoses Book VI [161]

Athens, the heart of Greece, was on the verge of capture by the barbarians. All hope was about to fail when Tereus, the young hero of Thrace, fought valiantly. He defended the city and drove off the enemy. Tereus was believed to be the son of Ares himself. King Pandion of Athens was pleased with the hero. An alliance was forged between Athens and Thrace. Pandion gave his eldest daughter in marriage to Tereus. Unfortunately, Hera and the three Graces did not attend the wedding. Now Hera was the goddess of marriage, wealth, fertility and prosperity. The three Graces gave their gifts of joy, beauty and fertility in every marriage. So you can see what their absence invoked. As an added measure, the wedding was attended by the Furies who held the bridal torch. A scritch owl[18] howled in the bridal chamber. Soon Procne gave birth to a boy named Itys. They were happy for five years.

Procne missed her young sister Philomela. She told her husband, "My dear, I dearly wish to see my sister. Either permit me to visit her. Or bring her here to Thrace for a short stay." Tereus prepared his ship and set sail to Athens. King Pandion welcomed him with good cheer. A grand feast was announced and Tereus told Pandion why he had come. Just then, Philomela walked in, dressed all in green silk like a nymph at play. She was even more beautiful than Procne - a beauty not of mortal kind. Tereus was flamed up and willing to commit treason to get her. He said, "I can't wait to take her home . . .my wife can't wait to see her." Pandion was a fool. He took Tereus' words to mean no harm. Philomela couldn't wait to see her sister as well. Soon she was on Tereus' ship, sailing far from Athens and her home.

As soon as the ship touched the shores of Thrace, Tereus seized Philomela and took her to his small stone cabin deep in the woods. She screamed and prayed but no one came to rescue her. Tereus raped her but she knew how to fight. She said, "O you beast! You have broken your oaths to my father and my sister! O savage horror! But you will be punished for what you have done. I'll tell the world how you raped me. I'll tell every rock, every stone my story." Tereus' anger rose like a forest fire. He drew his sword from its scabbard, seized Philomela by the hair and bound her arms. He pulled her tongue out and sliced it off, its roots still beating and quivering on the floor. The tongue coiled and lashed out on the floor much like a black serpent. Then Tereus renewed his pleasure on her wounded mutilated body.

Procne was waiting for her sister. When Tereus entered her chamber, she asked him where she was. He lied, sobbed and told her that Philomela had died in Athens. Procne tore off her hair and dressed in black. She raised a sepulchre in memory of her sister. Tereus offered his guilty prayer to the departed spirit. Twelve years passed in misery. Poor Philomela couldn't escape as Tereus had posted guards outside the stone cabin. She couldn't scream for help. There was an old loom in the cottage and that gave her an idea. She found some faded old wool and sprung them across the loom. She wove a tapestry of her plight. When it was done, she gave it to the maid who visited her once in a while. She explained to the maid that it was a gift for the queen through her gestures. The frail old woman delivered it to Procne. The queen went silent after opening the tapestry. There was nothing but anger. Vengeance. Blood and more vengeance. Tereus must feel vengeance and have a taste of his own blood, literally.

It was the Bacchanalia and the whole of Thrace was in a celebration. Procne dressed like a maenad[19], her hair wild, deerskin clinging to her chest and a light spear in her left hand. She rode her charger into the woods and found the cabin. The guard ran away when he saw a maenad standing before him. These maenads were prone to sudden drunken fury and ripped apart anyone who stood before them. Procne broke the cottage door, took her sister and dressed her as a maenad. Philomela was embarrassed to look at Procne. She trembled in her sister's arms while Procne mused over vengeance. Procne said, "Now is no time for tears. Let vengeance dance! We need good steel, my dear. Good steel and the tyrant's blood."

Young Itys was playing by and Procne saw him. She saw Tereus' sin in the boy. She did not want a son with that monster. But when the little boy ran to her and kissed her, her maternal instinct took over. But no! Vengeance must be had! "I am the daughter of Pandion, a true king. But my sister cannot speak. I cannot honour the throne of Tereus. It is total perversion!" she said. She seized Itys much like a tigress seizing a young deer. The boy screamed but Procne gagged him. She took him to her chamber. She unsheathed her dagger and ran it down his chest, stabbing his heart. She cut him into pieces and boiled some in a pot, the rest roasted on a spit. The floor ran blood.

Tereus sat at the table for the Bacchanalia banquet. Procne served him some "exotic" dishes. He relished the meat and asked, "Where is Itys?"

"He's inside," she said.

"Inside, where?" he asked again.

"Inside you." came the reply. "You ate the boy," she said calmly. And as she said this, Philomela walked into the room, her hair wild and spotted with Itys' blood. She flung the boy's head over Tereus' plate. He screamed in shock and gazed at the two Furies standing by him. They laughed and chased him out. As they ran behind him, they became birds. Procne became the sparrow. Philomela turned into a nightingale. Tereus himself became a plover, ready to fight.

CHAPTER FIFTEEN

JASON AND THE GOLDEN FLEECE

"'. . . Now to his rescue:
Great bulls will burn him blind with fiery breath,
And from the seeds that fall from his own hand
An army sprung from earth will strike him down
And he'll be fed as carrion to a dragon.'" Ovid,
Metamorphoses Book VII [168]

Long ago, there was a fight for power, a fight between two kings over the kingdom of Iolcus in Thessaly. Pelais, son of Poseidon, claimed the throne. Aeson was the rightful king. Pelias killed all of Aeson's children. Alcimede, Aeson's wife, gave birth to a baby boy just as Pelias marched into the castle. She arranged the maids to stand around the baby and weep as though it was still-born. This convinced Pelias and he left the child alone. That child was Jason, our hero for this wonderful tale of adventure, love and revenge.

Pelias ruled Iolcus with a heavy heart. There was an ancient prophecy. A man with one sandal would bring about the end of Pelias. Alcimede was afraid that Pelias might find Jason. So she sent him away to Master Chiron, the Centaur. Remember him, from "The Healer Who Gave Life to the Dead"? Yes, that's right, he raised Aesculapius. Now he raised Jason who grew up to be a skilled swordsman. Many years later, he returned to Iolcus on the day Pelias held the games of Poseidon. Jason had lost his sandal while wading through a river. Pelias trembled when he saw Jason with one sandal! Jason knew his past from Chiron. So he marched straight up to Pelias and said, "I come for my birthright. This throne is mine!"

"It is yours if you prove yourself worthy. Bring me the Golden Fleece and you shall have it!" said Pelias. The Golden Fleece was the prized possession of Aeetes, the King of Colchis. He had set a gigantic dragon to guard it. Pelias knew Aeetes would never part with it. The quest was on.

Jason announced the quest and several worthy heroes joined him. The skilled Argus made an excellent ship under the divine guidance of Athena. He made the mast with Zeus' sacred oak, a magic tree that could guide Jason during distress. Tiphys volunteered to be the helmsman. Other heroes included Hercules, Castor, Polydeuces, Peleus, Idmon the Seer, Meleager, Orpheus and many more. Atalanta, the huntress of Arcadia, was the only woman warrior in the team. Some of these would be the parents of heroes who fought in the Trojan War. The ship was named "Argo" and the heroes were called Argonauts.

The Argonauts had many adventures before reaching the island of Colchis. They had affairs with the women on the Isle of Lemnos, killed the Giant king Cyzicus, rescued Phineus from the harpies and got through the famous crashing rocks called the Symplegades. Jason himself had a minor affair with Queen Hypsipyle of Lemnos. But these are tales in themselves and we will not talk about them here. Jason arrived at the court of King Aeetes and claimed the Golden Fleece. The king agreed to give it to him if he performed three tasks the next day. They were

1. Yoke and plough a field with fire-breathing oxen - these were monstrous and unkillable. They couldn't be controlled either.
2. Sow the teeth of a dragon. An army will emerge from the teeth. This army will try to kill Jason.
3. Make the sleepless dragon guarding the fleece fall asleep.

Jason knew he was finished. How could he plough a field with fire-breathing oxen? He would be burned to death. If he did escape, he would be killed by the dragon-teeth army. And the third task was impossible to finish. It was the "sleepless" dragon! How to make the "sleepless" dragon fall asleep?

But Jason had another way. He had fallen in love with Medea, daughter of King Aeetes, the princess of Colchis. Now Medea was not an ordinary woman; she was a sorceress, a priestess of the goddess Hecate. Medea thought to herself, "A godlike power rules me, a power greater than all the gods! I will be known as the only woman who rescued heroes. Now to summon my higher intellect!" She walked toward the shrine of Hecate, an ancient altar in a deep forest. She saw Jason on the way. He told her, "My love, I desperately need your help. They say that you have powers. Please unleash them for me."

"My arts are to save your life. Only promise that you will marry me," she said. Jason swore an oath in the holy name of Hecate, the three-faced goddess of magic. She gave him a spray of magic herbs and he went back to his quarters. Dawn broke and crowds filled the arena of Aeetes, eager to watch Jason being torn to pieces by the fire-breathing oxen. Jason marched in with ease. The bulls roared at him and the ground shook with their approach. The Argonauts left their front-row seats in fear. Jason had smeared the magic herbs upon himself. The bulls became docile when he neared them and allowed themselves to be yoked. He ploughed much to the surprise of the Colchians. The Argonauts cheered their captain.

The next task was to defeat an army born from dragon teeth. Jason thrust his hands into a bronze helmet and sowed the serpent's teeth behind the plough. The teeth sizzled green like acid and burrowed into the soil. Suddenly, they sprouted and fully armed soldiers sprung from them. They clashed their weapons and were ready to slaughter the hero. Medea grew white with fear. She summoned up her courage and breathed a chant to Hecate. Jason, acting upon her advice, threw a rock into the army. Medea's chant made the soldiers attack the rock and kill each other in the process. The last trial was to face the sleepless dragon. This monster was heavily plumed, its skin was tougher than any armour and its triple tongue curled around deadly fangs. Jason walked up to the dragon and sprayed a green liquor distilled from Lethe's water, specially prepared by Medea during the dark moon phase. The dragon fell asleep and Jason returned victoriously with the Golden Fleece.

King Aeetes romped around his chamber in fury. How could Jason win! Just then, to add fuel to the fire, his guards informed him that Jason was sailing back with Medea aboard his ship. Furthermore, Medea was accompanied by Apsyrtus, her brother and son of Aeetes. Apsyrtus was a great warrior and had brought victory in many battles. How could he betray his father for his sister! The Golden Fleece and his children gone! Aeetes boarded his galley and gave chase. The cunning Medea saw him from a distance. She stabbed her brother Apsyrtus, chopped him into pieces and threw them overboard. King Aeetes could not see the sight! He slowed down to collect his son's remains while Jason steered away.

While the Argo sailed steadily, Jason heard a voice from the deck. He was surprised to find the mast, made of the sacred oak of Zeus, talking to him.

"Halt Jason! You shall not reach home for you have committed many sins on your quest to get the Golden Fleece. You have killed the innocent Apsyrtus!," it said in a voice that sounded like a nail being scraped down a piece of glass.

"What can I do, O holy wood of Zeus?" he asked.

"You and the Argonauts must be cleansed. Go to Aeaea, the island home of the great sorceress Circe[20], sister of Aeetes. She will cleanse you. Only then you may sail home," the mast sang loud and clear.

Jason plotted a course to Aeaea immediately. When they reached the island, the Argonauts found it a beautiful haven for herbs and beasts. Circe was bathing in a tide pool surrounded by wild animals. She had charmed them all to be her familiars. At once, she noticed Medea and invited the Argonauts into her cave. When Medea showed her the sword still red with the blood of Apsyrtus, Circe understood that they had come to be absolved of murder. Medea told her all of their adventure except the murder but Circe was even more powerful. She understood Medea's cunning. She caught a young pig, slit its throat with a ritual knife and caught the blood in a goblet. Then she chanted and poured the blood on everyone, cleansing them of their sin. Circe hated Jason for all his disloyalty and treachery. However, she was related to Medea and so she sent them off without any trouble.

The Argo sailed on smoothly and came to the island of the Sirens[21]. Orpheus[22], one of the Argonauts, had the gift of divine music. He played his lyre and the Sirens jumped back to hear songs sweeter than their own. When they reached Crete, guarded by the bronze giant Talos, Medea once again used her sorcery to kill the giant. Finally, Jason and Medea reached Iolcus in victory. Pelias stepped down and Jason became the rightful ruler of his father's kingdom. There was peace for a long time. But nothing lasts forever and Jason was a wicked man at heart, though heroic in temperament. His disloyalty caused a whole bunch of problems, but that's a story in itself.

CHAPTER SIXTEEN

THE ELIXIR OF ETERNAL YOUTH

"'A magic, potent drink that dissipates
Old age and fills old veins with manly blood -'" Ovid,
Metamorphoses Book VII [174]

Jason's victory and ascension were celebrated by all of Greece. The castle was full of rich gifts and incense. A gold-horned bull was sacrificed to celebrate the bringing of the Golden Fleece. Greek temples blazed with sacrificial flames for many days. But old Aeson did not join the celebration. He was very sick and almost dying in his bed. Jason was all gloom and doom. He approached Medea and said, "O wife, dearest one, you have saved me. I owe you more than anyone. If your arts are capable of so much, what can't they do? Please take some years of my life and give them to my father! I beg you, please rejuvenate him!" His face was wet with tears.

"What is this, my husband? How can I give another man one minute of your precious life? Hecate will not grant me that kind of power nor can I ask her for such crimes. This borders on necromancy! I will do something else to please you. I know of old magic that revives the flesh and increases the days of men," she said. Jason was glad and left her alone to practise her arts.

Three nights later, Medea walked into the forest, loose-cloaked and barefoot, her hair falling over her naked breasts. The moon was full and the entire forest shone in silver splendour. She reached a clearing and put down her tools. She cleansed herself in moon water thrice and cast a magic circle. Then she fell upon her knees to Hecate, praying thus: "O Night! Mistress of darkness! Lady of potions and poisons! O you, Hecate, who knows our untold desires and works our will, mistress of our secret spells, come to my call! When you've entered me, my power makes winds vanish or return! My spells have torn the throats of dragons, overturned the tide and demolished the mountains! Ghosts fall under my command as you, my lady of the moon, make even the dawn tremble. O Hecate, now I need your aid: a magic, potent drink that dissipates old age and grants youth. Guide me, my queen!" Medea boarded her special chariot pulled by dragons and vanished into the sky.

Medea flew in her chariot for nine days, collecting ingredients for the Elixir of Youth as guided by Hecate. She cut herbs even from Mt. Olympus with her bronze scimitar. She took roots and rare grasses from dangerous mountains and valleys. She even collected seaweed from the darkest depths of the sea. Finally, she returned home, her dragons tired. The fumes from the herbs had scorched them and they had to shed their scales! She started working straight away. Jason left her alone knowing full well the horrific nature of her midnight rituals. He only wanted results. The process didn't matter to him.

When the moon was dark, Medea made two altars outside her castle. The right one, she consecrated to Hecate and the left to Youth. She decked her altars with the herbs she had gathered. She dug a moat and slit the throat of a black sheep, letting its blood flow down the altar into her cauldron. She mixed warm milk and wine into the cauldron. The chant began and at once, the cauldron began bubbling and gurgling. Medea began wailing her chants to Hades and Hecate. It was a sight too horrible for words to describe. The cauldron became quiet and she ordered her servants to bring old Aeson. She closed his eyes with a strange lullaby and placed him upon the altar of Youth. She commanded Jason and the others to close their eyes and never look at her dark rites. Medea dipped branches into the sheep's blood and lit torches. She cleansed the old man's flesh thrice with fire, thrice with water and thrice with smouldering sulphur.

Medea's magic cauldron began bubbling once again. Now she threw in the magic herbs, precious stones from the Orient, sands from out of oyster shells, the white frost of the sea scooped under the full moon, wings of the scritch owl, intestines of the werewolf, the scaled skin of a water-snake, liver of a long-lived deer, rotten eggs, the battered head of a cow that had lived for eight hundred years and many other things that cannot be named. The froth boiled on the surface of the cauldron and the potion turned an acidic green. When the potion was ready, Medea dipped a withered olive branch into the cauldron and pulled it out! And lo! The branch hung rich with olives and leaves! Some of the foam spilled on the earth below and the soil became rich with fertile vegetation!

The brew was ripe and Medea knew it was time. She flashed her dagger and slit Aeson's throat. She drained his body of blood and poured the steaming potion into his mouth. The results were instant. The old man's grey hair became black and wavy. His wrinkles vanished, his teeth renewed and he became strong and muscular. Aeson was dazed at himself, looking forty years younger! The joyful Bacchus saw her at work and exacted a promise from Medea. He wanted his early nurses restored to their youthful beauty and Medea accepted. Such was her power! But even more was her fury!

The daughters of Pelias (the man who ruled Iolcus before Jason) saw Aeson and wanted the same magic performed for their father. It is alright to trust your foe-turned-friend, but this trust must have certain limits. Three days later, Medea prepared a weak brew of old impotent herbs. She wanted revenge on her husband's former enemy. The cauldron bubbled and the fire burned. Old Pelias was brought out by his daughters. Medea commanded them to slit his throat and empty his blood so she could fill his body with the Elixir of Youth. They eagerly cut him up, eyes closed, clothed with his blood and ignored his pleas. Once the deed was done, Medea slit his throat and tossed his mangled remains into boiling water. She jumped into her winged chariot and flew away, laughing into the night!

Later, Pelias' son, Acastus, drove away Jason and Medea into exile for murdering his father. Jason was not bothered as he got back to his father. He and Medea settled down in Corinth, quite happy with their vengeance. They had two sons and lived in peace. But the wheel of fortune turned for all and bad times were just ahead.

CHAPTER SEVENTEEN

MEDEA'S BRIDAL GIFTS

"... There Medea found
Jason remarried, and with her deadly spells
She burnt his bride to ashes while two seas
Witnessed the flames that poured from Jason's halls."
Ovid, *Metamorphoses* Book VII [179]

Medea, like most sorceresses, went away on long tours in the middle of the night and returned many months later. Jason knew this and never cared to ask her whereabouts. Once, Medea was away on a long trip collecting herbs and stones. She was away for a really long time. When she returned to Corinth, she found Jason engaged to Creusa, daughter of Creon, the King of Corinth. What more? Medea was to be exiled before the marriage! She confronted him right away.

"I'm away and what do I find when I return? My husband engaged to the young princess of Corinth! You traitor! Have you forgotten your oaths to me? Have you forgotten your oaths to Hecate? Do not forget that it was I who saved you. I made you king of Iolcus. I helped you get revenge on Pelias. I sacrificed my brother for you! I left my father and betrayed him for you! Where is your love? Or your loyalty? You should thank me for making you a hero!" she stormed at him.

"You have a right to be angry, O wife. But I did this to secure land and titles for our sons. And I don't have to thank you. You have to thank Aphrodite for falling in love with me. You're a savage woman. Your customs are not ours. You have no kingdom nor titles for our sons. What do you think they'll inherit, magic? Don't be a fool!" he said.

"What about my exile? Why do I have to leave my sons?" she wept.

"That was the condition set by Creon if I was to marry his daughter. The boys will be brought up in our Greek ways. You may go back to Colchis, your homeland," he said.

"But how can I go back? I am a murderer and traitor in Colchis because I slew my brother for you!" she yelled.

"Then you can go anywhere in that chariot of yours. Just leave us in peace!" he said.

"I know full well what you are up to. You want to be king of Corinth, don't you? You lust after the young princess, don't you? You are not doing this for our sons! You are a selfish, ambitious and greedy monster...far worse than the dragon guarding the Golden Fleece!" she roared like a lioness being hunted.

"Off with you, you witch! Guards, take her away!" Jason ordered the guards. But Medea walked away quietly.

Inflamed with anger, hatred and disgust, Medea made an altar to Hecate once again. Jason must be taught a lesson. He was a weak-minded traitor and a fool to scorn her, the priestess of Hecate! Savage indeed! She was not 'savage' when she helped him get the Golden Fleece! What cruelty to separate her from her children! Magic must not be meddled with and Jason was about to fall into the darkest hell. She brought out her cauldron and concocted a deadly poison. This she sprayed on her silk gown and diadem. Then she folded it, placed the diadem on top and placed the gifts into a golden box. She took the box to Jason.

"What now, Medea? What's this?" he asked.

"I have accepted my fate for our sons' sake. Please send these gifts to Creusa, the future queen of Corinth and mother to my sons," she said timidly.

"And will you leave us in peace? You are, of course, invited to the wedding, should you wish to come," he said without a heart.

"No, I have other plans. I'll leave after seeing my sons one last time," she said.

The gifts were taken to young Creusa who screamed in joy to see such a beautiful gown. It was Medea's own golden gown woven by master weavers. The fine gold thread reflected the rays of the sun. And the diadem was of red gold, beaming with diamonds and rubies. Creusa wore the dress and the diadem. She appeared as beautiful as Aurora but just for a moment. Then she began screaming in pain because the dress had stuck to her skin and had started melting her alive. The diadem sunk into her skull and she dropped dead into a puff of smoke and liquid flesh. Nothing remained except her skeleton and the red gold frame of the diadem stuck to a skull with the eyes melted down. Creon rushed to her aid and tried to remove the dress. He too melted away in the process.

Meanwhile, Medea was shown to her sons playing in Creon's throne room. She caught them both and slit their throats. She believed that death was far better than being enslaved or sold to someone's army. Jason would do that because they were 'savage' boys. Bathed in her children's blood, she called her chariot and flew away, leaving a trail of blood and tears behind. As he had broken his vows to Medea, the vows sworn in the name of Hecate, Jason lived and died all alone. When he became very old, he found the old tattered remains of the Argo and slept under it. The mast crashed over him and killed him instantly. Medea went on to marry Aegeus, the King of Athens and form cults of Hecate. Today she is a symbol of feminist power often used to symbolise the independent woman.

CHAPTER EIGHTEEN

KING MINOS AND SCYLLA

"The girl came gliding where her father slept,
And clipped (O fatal error of her will!)
The purple plume whose secret was his life.
Wearing that plume (since she was sure of welcome)
She strode to Minos' camp and stood before him." Ovid,
Metamorphoses Book VIII [199]

Once there was a powerful king named Minos of Crete. He was the son of Zeus and Europa; the first king to build a powerful navy. He had sent his son Androgeos to participate in the Athenian Games conducted by King Aegeus of Athens. Androgeos won all the competitions and this made his opponents green with envy. They ambushed him on the way back and killed him. Minos was enraged as Aegeus had done nothing to save his boy. He was on his way to Athens to avenge the death of his son. King Nisus of Megara, brother of Aegeus, refused to allow him passage and Minos decided to conquer his land.

Megara put up a strong defence and Minos could not enter its secure walls. Apparently, Nisus had a purple plume bound to his hair. This talisman protected the city from invaders. King Nisus had a daughter named Scylla. She used to climb the city's highest tower and drop stones down to hear the echoes they made. As her father was out fighting, she climbed the tower and saw the enemy. She saw the shining shield of Minos, his purple plume upon his engraved helmet, and the way he threw a spear and stood dazzled by his strength and skill. And when he drew his bow, it was as if Apollo himself had taken his weapon. She fell in love with the king of their enemy.

Scylla saw Minos fight every day. She saw his white tent at night and wondered what he would say if she visited him. Minos was a just man; he fought for his son. So he would understand her and perhaps, take her with him. As dawn broke, she stepped into her father's chamber. She took his dagger and clipped the purple plume from his hair. Poor Nisus transformed into an eagle as he lost his precious possession. Wearing the plume, she marched out to Minos' camp. She stood before the dazed enemy and said, "Love guided me. My name is Scylla, daughter of Nisus. Here's my dowry - the plume, my country's wealth and security. It's all yours now. Only take me as your wife." She threw the plume to Minos who shuddered.

"I hope the very gods in heaven send curses on you for your treachery. Nor shall I take you to Crete because a woman who betrayed once will do it again," said Minos. He walked away from her in disgust. He left Megara and sailed back to Crete. Scylla went mad with grief and cursed Minos from her tower. "O son of Europa! Your wife Pasiphaë would give birth to a monster - half man, half bull! She will be unfaithful to you! You have failed to sacrifice the best bull for Poseidon! The sea god's curse will make your wife mate with a bull! Your kingdom will be destroyed by your monster son!" she yelled aloud and jumped into the sea. She became the sea bird ciris and tried to fly over Minos' boat. But her father (the eagle) caught her and held her.

Minos knew full well that he had failed to sacrifice his best bull to Poseidon. It was required of him every year. He had kept the best for himself and sacrificed another bull to Poseidon, for which the god was angry. He also knew that his wife Pasiphaë was a sorceress who practised the dark arts. She was the daughter of Helios and sister of Circe. (So yes, Medea was her niece - you may notice that all these powerful sorceresses are in some way related to Helios, the sun). Just as Scylla cursed, Poseidon made Pasiphaë fall in love with the best bull, the one Minos failed to sacrifice. In his absence, the sorceress arranged for the architect Daedalus to construct a hollow wooden cow. She went into the hollow cow and mated with the bull. By the time Minos reached Crete, she had given birth to Asterion, a horrific creature with the body of a man and the head of a bull. He was later known as the Minotaur or the Bull of Minos. He ate naught but human flesh. So Minos had an idea.

CHAPTER NINETEEN

THE LABYRINTH OF CRETE

"... His naked arms
Whirled into wind; his lips, still calling out
His father's name, were gulfed in the dark sea." Ovid,
Metamorphoses Book VIII [204]

Daedalus was the greatest architect of Athens. He lived with his sons Icarus and Iapyx. He also had a nephew named Talos who he took as his apprentice. However, Daedalus was jealous of Talos' ingenuity in using fishbones as a saw. Daedalus tried to kill Talos by pushing him off a steep hill. But Athena caught the boy and transformed him into a partridge. Daedalus was caught, tried and sentenced to death. He escaped and fled to Crete where Minos hired him to construct the masts for his ships. In his absence, Daedalus had made the hollow wooden cow for Pasiphaë, the queen of Crete.

Minos summoned Daedalus and Icarus to his court. When they came, he said, "I know that you built the hollow cow for my wife. But I did not call you to punish you. Your services are still required. Build me a maze, the largest one ever built in Greece. Place my son, the Minotaur, inside the maze." Daedalus and Icarus were amazed at the proposal but accepted it. They wanted to show off their skill. Little did they know that Minos held his grudge. Daedalus constructed the Labyrinth, a maze that meandered like a river, twisting through and through. Only the cleverest mind could ever find an exit from that maze. The Labyrinth was constructed and the Minotaur was placed inside. Minos still wanted his revenge from Athens, because his son had died fighting a bull there. And Athens was struck with the plague. An oracle had asked the people to obey the commands of Minos if they wanted to survive the plague. Minos commanded the king of Athens to send seven boys and seven girls once every nine years to feed the Minotaur.

Once the job was done, Minos imprisoned Daedalus and Icarus in the island of Knossos so that they would keep his secrets. This was his punishment for building the hollow cow for his wife. Daedalus saw the birds flying over him. He collected the feathers that had fallen around the island and melted some wax. He made two pairs of large wings much like the birds. He tied these 'wings' around the arms of his son and taught him how to use them. Father and son took off and flew happily imitating the birds. But Icarus got too close to the sun. He flew higher and higher in his ecstasy, not listening to the words of his father. The sun melted the wax and the feathers fell off. Soon Icarus tumbled and fell into the sea. Daedalus saw nothing but a splash. He rushed towards his fallen son. But Icarus was already dead. Daedalus fished the boy from the sea and buried him in a grave nearby. The place where the boy fell is called the Icarian Sea. This was Daedalus' punishment for killing his nephew. So the Wheel of Fortune turns, bringing today's results from yesterday's actions.

CHAPTER TWENTY

THE SON OF THE HEIRLESS KING

"Meanwhile young Theseus came in full disguise;
Not even Father Aegeus recognized him.
He, a soldierly young man, had forced
Peace on that strip of land between two seas." Ovid,
Metamorphoses Book VII [180]

King Aegeus of Athens was known for his diplomacy and strength. He was the founder of Athens and hence a part of the Mediterranean is called the Aegean Sea. Nisus and Lycus were his two brothers. He ruled the region of Attica, giving Megara to Nisus and Euboea to Lycus. Aegeus was married to two queens but none of them gave birth to any children. Later he married Aethra, daughter of King Pittheus of Troezen. Though he had everything his heart desired, he was barren. He was even nicknamed the "heirless king". He consulted the Oracle of Delphi and got an answer that he would have an heir not of his blood. Queen Aethra was visited by Poseidon and she became pregnant. She gave birth to Theseus, the hero of Athens.

But Aethra remained in Troezen to take care of the boy and Aegeus went back to Athens. There he met Medea, who had just arrived from Corinth with the blood of her sons still on her hands. Aegeus married Medea right away. They had a son named Medus.

Young Theseus was brought up in Troezen and grew up to be a fine warrior. When he came of age, his mother told him that he was the heir to the throne of Athens. Theseus could reach Athens safely by taking a ship but he chose the dangerous chthonic[23] path to test his mettle. The land route from Troezen to Athens had what was then called the Six Gates of the Underworld, each guarded by a chthonic monster. Theseus met all of them as follows:

1. Gate of Aesculapius - this was guarded by the club-wielding giant Periphetes. Theseus defeated him and took his club.
2. Gate of Isthmus - Theseus slew the giant Sinis by tearing him apart. He also seduced his daughter Perigune.
3. Gate of Crommyon - the hero slew the enormous Crommyonian Sow
4. Gate of Megara - Theseus killed the guardian and bandit Sciron
5. Gate of Eleusis - Theseus beat King Cercyon at a wrestling match and killed him
6. Gate of Procrustes - Procrustes was another demon who killed people by stretching them or cutting off their feet to fit into his beds. Theseus killed him by stretching him and then cutting off his head. Together, these six adventures are called the Six Labours of Theseus.

When Theseus reached Athens, he disguised himself as a beggar. He went to the court of Aegeus but Medea recognized him instantly. She was worried that Aegeus might choose Theseus over her son Medus. She made him accept a challenge - that of killing the Marathonian Bull. This was the famed white bull of Poseidon. Hercules tried to capture it as part of his twelve labours[24] but the bull broke loose and wandered into Marathon. Theseus captured the bull and sacrificed it in honour of Athena and Apollo. Medea's plan failed and she decided to kill Theseus herself. She mixed poison in his wine goblet and offered it to him as a drink of victory. Aegeus recognised the hero at the last moment and knocked the goblet before Theseus brought it to his lips. Ashamed and afraid, Medea flew to Asia in her dragon chariot.

CHAPTER TWENTY-ONE

THESEUS AND THE MINOTAUR

"Where other heroes failed, the son of Aegeus,
Led by young Ariadne, walked the maze,
And winding up the thread that guided him,
Raped Minos' daughter and sailed off with her." Ovid,
Metamorphoses Book VIII [202]

The whole of Athens went into celebration over the victories of young Theseus. King Aegeus was still gloomy and refused to revel. Theseus walked to his father, goblet in hand and spoke thus, "Hail King! O mighty father! Why do you sit in sorrow? Who don't you drink the elixir of Bacchus and make merry?"

"My dear son! The joy of my life! I'm joyous of your victories, make no mistake about that. But a real king does not drink when his people are subject to ruin," Aegeus said.

"What ruin are you speaking of father?" questioned the hero.

"My son, Athens has to send seven boys and seven girls to the Minotaur every nine years to appease King Minos of

Crete. I failed to rescue his son. Now my sons and daughters face my sin," he wept for the loss of his subjects.

"Have no fear, father. It's my duty to protect the Athenians. I will sail to Crete and slay this Minotaur. This will be my quest," said Theseus.

"O no, my son. I have just found you. I will not lose the heir to the Athenian throne!" said Aegeus.

"Don't worry, father. Trust in my strength. I have Poseidon's blood in my veins. Let me dress as one of the seven boys and go with the sacrificial party. Upon my return, I will hoist the white sail to indicate my success. It will be the white sail, I am sure," said Theseus with full confidence.

Aegeus trembled as he helped Theseus wear the ordinary Athenian garb and join the sacrificial party. They boarded a lonely ship with black sails and sailed away to Crete. Once Theseus and the others reached Crete, Minos' guards stripped them of all weapons. Ariadne, daughter of Minos, had come to look at the sacrifice being prepared for the Minotaur as was the custom. She saw Theseus and fell in love with him. Ariadne wept as Theseus would soon be devoured by the Minotaur. She gave him a ball of silk thread. Theseus would unwind the thread as he walked through the maze and follow the thread to get out. And as all tales go, Theseus promised to marry her if he got out alive.

Minos' guards walked the Athenians into the maze. Some of them were weeping and trembling. The guards unsheathed their swords and pointed them at the victims, forcing them to go inside. It was death, either way. Theseus pulled out Ariadne's thread and walked to the centre of the maze. He found the monster and a terrific fight ensued. Theseus choked the beast with his strength. Then he followed the string and broke out of the Labyrinth. Theseus took Ariadne on his ship and sailed away to Athens. However, he broke his promise (much like Jason and the other 'heroes') to her on the Isle of Dia. He left her sleeping and sailed on to more adventures. When Ariadne woke up, she saw that everyone had left her. She was afraid, alone, lost and miserable. Her heart was broken. She walked towards a brook to drink water. As she dropped tears into the brook, she observed a handsome man, his hair bound with grape leaves, looking at her. He was Bacchus, the god of wine and revelry. Bacchus married Ariadne and gave her a wedding present - a tiara of stars that became the constellation Corona Borealis.

CHAPTER TWENTY-TWO

MELEAGER AND THE CALYDONIAN BOAR

"When Althaea lay in childbirth with Meleager,
The three Fates tossed a bit of fuel to fire,
And as they spun the taut-bound threads of life
They chanted, 'Just as long as this wood burns,
So long, O precious child, your life shall last.'" Ovid,
Metamorphoses Book VIII [211]

The city of Calydon was tormented by a demonic boar, a colossal beast that had fiery eyes and smokey breath. Its neck was of iron, its bristles sharp as spears and its skin impenetrable by any weapon. This beast was sent by Artemis herself in revenge. Oeneus, King of Calydon, had raised altars to every deity and gave them holy offerings. He had offered grain to Ceres, wine to Bacchus and olive oil to Athena. But the altars of Artemis stood dusty and neglected. The huntress of the wild was enraged and had sent the boar to teach Oeneus a lesson. The Calydonian farmers lined up at Oeneus' court to complain - the boar had trampled the crops, breathed fire over the vegetables, blackened boughs and slaughtered the cattle. Meleager, the young prince of Calydon and son of Oeneus, stood up to defeat the boar and bring peace to the land.

Meleager had a dark prophecy the night he was born. When Queen Althaea (wife of Oeneus and mother of Meleager) went into labour, the Moirai[25] appeared. The three Fates looked at a bough burning in the fireplace and spun out the threads of Meleager's fate. They said, "The boy will live as long as this stick burns." Althaea took the burning stick out of the fire and dipped it into water. She bound the stick and put it away. That was a long time ago. Now Meleager wanted to hunt the boar and Althaea hoped the stick would not endanger him. Anyway, Meleager announced his quest and a host of young heroes joined him. Theseus, Jason, Castor, Polydeuces, Peleus, Nestor, Laertes, Caeneus and many others came to prove their strength. Castor and Polydeuces were the twin sons of Tyndareus and Leda. They were brothers of Helen of Troy and Clytemnestra. Peleus was the father of Achilles and Nestor was advisor to the Greeks during the Trojan War. Laertes was the father of Odysseus and Caeneus was the hero who was once a woman. Last of all came Atalanta, the only woman warrior to join Meleager's team.

Atalanta was the famed virgin huntress of Arcadia, daughter of King Iasus. She had been one of the Argonauts. Iasus was disappointed when Atalanta was born. So he took his infant daughter and abandoned her in a forest. A she-bear found the child and suckled her. Atalanta was taken by a group of hunters and raised in their tradition. She learned to hunt with her bow and live in the ways of Artemis. She wore a loose cloak held by a polished brooch. Her hair was trimmed and drawn back in a single twist in the fashion of male hunters. An ivory quiver swung from her left shoulder. She held a longbow in her left hand. She looked like a young boy but talked gracefully like a maiden. But she was no softie. She had killed centaurs. She once fought with Peleus (father of Achilles) in a wrestling match and she won. She had also fought in many wars and was recognized as the hero of Arcadia. Meleager fell in love with her at first sight.

The hunting party went deep into the Calydonian forest. Some of the heroes set traps for the boar. Others took out their nets and sharpened their swords. Some followed their hounds to a swamp hidden under willows and reeds. The mighty boar jumped out from behind the reeds and ambushed them. He impaled the hounds with his huge tusks. The heroes' arrows were useless against his tough hide. The beast sharpened its tusks against a tree and charged at them. He sent Nestor and Jason sprawling into the swamp. Bold Atalanta ran like the wind and fired a flaming arrow from her bow. The arrow sped through the forest and pierced the boar behind its ear. The arrow went deep into the boar and Meleager shouted, "Honour to Atalanta for drawing first blood!" The men were furious and jealous. Finally, it was Meleager who killed the beast.

The Calydonian boar was dead and Meleager looked at Atalanta standing with her bow. He hailed her and said, "Dear huntress of Arcadia, you drew first blood in this hunt. The hide belongs to you!" He placed the boar's tough hide and its ferocious head near her feet. The huntress liked the gifts and of course, the giver too. But Meleager's uncles interfered. Plexippus and Toxeus were the brothers of Althaea and uncles to Meleager. They had participated in the hunt but didn't do anything heroic. They took the gifts offered to Atalanta and said, "A woman honoured with a hunter's spoils! Do not dishonour us Meleager." The young hero became so angry that he drew out his sword and killed them.

News came to Althaea in her palace. She was delighted that her son had won the hunt. But she was horrified that he had slain her brothers. She ordered her servants to build a huge fire with pine knots. Mother and sister fought in her. She said, "O triple goddesses! O mighty Furies of the night! How can I be happy when my brothers are dead? I cannot reward my son with my brothers' ghosts haunting me. How can I kill my own son? O child, whose life should've been smothered when the flaming stick burned, I saved you. Yet from what? Your victory is my curse!" She wailed and brought out the dampened stick that she had saved on the night Meleager was born. She threw it into the fire. Meleager had not yet returned from the forest. He was on the way back when he suddenly fell, his whole body burning. The flames reached his soul and he died crying the name of his mother with his last breath.

CHAPTER TWENTY-THREE

BAUCIS AND PHILEMON

"Shy Baucis spoke to him, 'Our dearest wish is
To be your servants in that marble temple,
And since we've lived together all our lives,
So may we share the moment of our death.'" Ovid,
Metamorphoses Book VIII [220]

Many aeons ago, in the foothills of Phrygia, there was a small cottage. Old wife Baucis lived with her husband Philemon there. They survived with the produce from their kitchen garden as Philemon was too old to farm. It so happened that Zeus the mighty thunderer and his son, Hermes, the wielder of the Caduceus[26] visited the town of Phrygia. They were disguised as merchants from abroad. They knocked at every door asking for food and shelter, and the door was slammed on their faces. "Let's teach these damned Phrygians a lesson, my boy," said Zeus. "There is still one more dwelling over there, father. We must try that too before we do anything rash," answered Maia's boy[27]. They saw a tiny cottage near the mountains, away from the bustling city. They went towards the cottage and knocked at the door.

Old Philemon answered the door. He was surprised and happy to receive strangers. There was only a low bench and a worn-out table. Philemon dusted the bench for the strangers. He laid an old but clean rug over it. Baucis stirred the dying fire and breathed over the coals. She reached into the rafters overhead and gathered some twigs. She placed these beneath her old copper pot hanging in the fireplace and started preparing supper. Baucis went to her kitchen garden and cut a cabbage. Philemon brought out some precious bacon stored for propitious times. They tossed these into the pot. The gods sat down and the table was brought. The table was shaking as one leg was shorter than the rest. Baucis placed an old cup beneath the leg and righted the table. She also rubbed the table with fragrant mint before laying supper.

"We be humble folk that dwell upon the gifts of our kitchen garden," said Philemon. "What you have is more than enough for us," said Zeus. First, they were offered Athena's fruit - the olive, as a token of welcome. Then Baucis brought fresh cherries, wine, sweet lettuce, cottage cheese, radishes and baked eggs. All of these were laid out on earthen bowls. Then they brought out the soup, which was the main course. Last of all there was dessert - nuts, figs, dates, apples, grapes and honey. But more than these, Baucis and Philemon cheered the guests with their good hearts. Once the soup bowl was empty, Philemon watched it fill itself. He was shocked. All the empty flasks were filling themselves with wine. The old couple understood who their divine guests were and raised their arms in reverence.

"We were about to annihilate this god-forsaken town. But you shall receive a gift, for your hospitality and your kindness," said Zeus. The old couple were asked to leave their home and go to the mountain. They watched Zeus call forth a huge storm. A flood rose over everything except their cottage. Their cottage transformed into a marble temple with a golden dome. "Ask anything and I will grant it!" said Zeus to the couple.

"Our dearest wish is to be your servants in that marble temple. Since we have lived together all our lives, we would like to share the moment of our death," said Baucis humbly. "I hope I never see my beloved wife's grave, nor she mine," added Philemon.

Zeus granted their wishes. Baucis and Philemon became his servants and watched over his temple. When the moment came for them to leave this world, Philemon saw Baucis turn into a tree. Philemon too transformed into a majestic tree. They entwined each other and seemed to grow from a single trunk. Such is the exalted state of those who revere the gods and show compassion to every creature in this short life.

CHAPTER TWENTY-FOUR

The Infant Who Strangled Serpents

"Then she went to tell Jove the son of Saturn, and
said, 'Father Jove, lord of the lightning—I have a word
for
your ear. There is a fine child born this day, Eurystheus,
son to Sthenelus the son of Perseus; he is of your
lineage;
it is well, therefore, that he should reign over the
Argives.'
'On this Jove was stung to the very quick, and in his
rage he caught Folly by the hair, and swore a great oath
that never should she again invade starry heaven and
Olympus, for she was the bane of all." Homer, *Iliad*
[500-01]

General Amphitryon of Thebes was a ferocious warrior,
one who dared fight the Teumessian Fox. He worked for

Creon, King of Thebes. He was also a descendant of the great hero Perseus. The Teumessian Fox was faster than the wind and impossible to catch. Amphitryon caught it with the help of his divine dog Laelaps. Next, he went away to fight the Taphians. In his absence, Zeus arrived at his castle in his guise. The mighty thunderer was in love with Alcmene, the beautiful wife of Amphitryon. He spent three days with Alcmene who thought the god was her husband. Amphitryon arrived later as the god left. This is going to be a bit weird, but true and all the facts must be mentioned when talking about myths, so here goes...Alcmene was pregnant with twins; one of them from Zeus and the other from Amphitryon.

Hera, queen of Mt. Olympus, and wife of the mighty Zeus, was extremely jealous of her husband's mortal lovers and their children. She often took her vengeance on the demigods born to her husband. Poor Alcmene was in labour but Hera commanded Ilithyia to prolong the labour. Ilithiya was the goddess of labour and she could not disobey Hera. But there was another master plan in this. Hera had asked her husband to promise that he would make the firstborn in the House of Perseus as king of Tiryns. Zeus agreed, hoping that it would be his son born to Alcmene. But Hera had another candidate in mind. That was why she prolonged Alcmene's labour to make her preferred candidate to be born first. This was Eurystheus, son of King Sthenelaus and Queen Nicippe. Sthenelaus was none other than the son of Perseus and Andromeda. He was also the uncle of Amphitryon. Anyway, poor Alcmene pleaded to Lucina, goddess of childbirth, to ease her pains and loosen her womb. But Lucina came and sat cross-legged at her threshold, aggravating her pain.

Alcmene was in labour for seven days and nights. She hoped she would die soon. Her red-haired maid, Galanthis, had an idea. She went to Lucina at the threshold and told her that her mistress had delivered a boy. Lucina was surprised and leaped to her feet. This eased Alcmene's womb and she delivered twins - Alcides (he was later called Hercules or Heracles in Greek) and Iphicles. Alcides was the demigod - son of Zeus and Iphicles was the son of Amphitryon. Lucina was furious. She held Galanthis by her red hair and turned her into a tiny weasel. Alcmene was afraid that her son might be killed by Hera. So she placed the baby into a basket and asked her maids to leave it in the forest. The goddess Athena found the baby and brought it to Hera herself, asking her to nurse the baby. Hera took pity on the baby and nursed him. But Alcides bit her breast and her milk splashed forth, forming the Milky Way galaxy (now there is a similar Egyptian myth where goddess Isis feeds the pharaoh with her milk). She pushed him away but Alcides had already gained the powers of the immortals. She gave the child to Athena who brought it back to Alcmene.

Hera understood it was Alcides who had drunk her milk. She was furious. Alcmene held a re-naming ceremony and gave the name of Hercules "Hera's pride" to her son to appease the goddess. But Hera simply could not be appeased. He and Iphicles were in their cradle when she sent two serpents to kill the children. Iphicles cried in fear but Hercules caught the serpents, each in one hand and strangled them. Amphitryon saw him playing with the dead serpents. He called in the famed Seer Tiresias who prophesied that Hercules would slay demons but suffer most. Hercules fought for King Creon against the Minyans. Creon was very pleased and gave his daughter Megara in marriage to Hercules. As predicted by Tiresias, Hercules had much suffering in his fate. Hera made him mad and out of fury, he killed his wife and his eight sons. He wailed aloud when he came out of madness. He ran away and consulted the Oracle of Delphi. Unbeknownst to him, the Oracle was seized by Hera and commanded him to go to King Eurystheus to get his crimes purified.

CHAPTER TWENTY-FIVE

The Twelve Labours of Hercules

"'My hands make better speeches
Than my tongue. Go try to win a battle
With your talk!'" Ovid, *Metamorphoses* Book IX [230]

Hercules was a criminal - he had committed the worst sin of killing his own blood. Even great heroes and kings were not exempt from crimes. They had to be exiled and purified by other kings or priests before they could enter their homeland again. Hercules went to Tiryns which was ruled by his cousin Eurystheus (it was actually his kingdom; the throne was given to Eurystheus by Hera). Eurystheus asked Hercules to perform ten impossible tasks to get purified. Later, after Hercules had done them, he added another two. He was a tricky little rat now, wasn't he?

The Nemean Lion

A hideous lion was ruining the city of Nemea. This lion had golden fur and razor-sharp claws sharper than any sword known to mankind. Its hide was impenetrable and its teeth were like iron. Hercules wandered about gathering arrows to kill the beast. When he met the lion, he shot the arrows and found them useless. The arrows slid off and broke apart when they hit the lion's tough hide. Finally, Hercules lured it into a cave. He blocked the entrance with a boulder and strangled the beast with his bare hands. Then he took the claws and used these to skin the beast. He appeared before the people of Nemea, wearing the hide. They sacrificed a ram to Zeus and celebrated the victory of Hercules. He returned to Tiryns on the thirtieth day, carrying the dead lion, wearing its hide around his waist. He was a formidable sight to see! Poor Eurystheus was terrified and ordered Hercules to display his spoils outside the city gates from then on. "Your labours will get tougher, now that you have proved yourself," he said. "Bring it on!" said Hercules. Eurystheus was not giving his throne up so easily.

The Lernaean Hydra

The hydra was a venomous five-headed colossal serpent that lived in Lake Lerna, a horrible place near the Underworld. The hydra's breath was poisonous and its blood was like acid. It was so deadly that even its smell was enough to kill mortals from a distance! And what more? If one of its heads was cut off, two grew up in its place. And it breathed fire! The hydra was a perfect killing machine. Hercules covered his nose and mouth before he approached the beast. He chopped off its head and knew it could not be killed as more heads grew back. He withdrew and prayed to Athena who gave him a golden sword. He also called his nephew Iolaus to assist him. Iolaus told him to cauterise the stumps of the beast after cutting the heads off. When Hera saw Hercules winning, she sent a huge crab to stop Hercules. The hero simply stomped on it and used the golden sword to cut the heads off of the hydra. Iolaus cauterised the stumps and the hydra was dead. Hera turned the crab into the constellation Cancer. Hercules dipped his arrows in the hydra's blood to be used for later labours.

The Ceryneian Hind

This was a fire-breathing female deer with golden antlers and bronze hooves. Eurystheus wanted Hercules to bring this beast alive. Hercules went to Ceryneia and found it impossible to catch because of its swiftness. Furthermore, the deer was sacred to Artemis. Hercules chased the deer for a year till it was tired and came down to a river, then he subdued it by forcing it into the water. He brought it to Artemis and asked her permission to carry it to Eurystheus as his third labour. The goddess consented and Eurystheus was shocked to see Hercules carrying the deer outside his city gates. This was the longest of all labours.

The Erymanthian Boar

This was a gigantic wild boar of immense strength. It was untameable and ruined the forests near Mt. Erymanthus. Hercules shouted loudly, confusing the boar and allowed it to run uphill. He jumped upon the huge beast's neck and pushed it into the snow on the mountain. Then he clubbed it and carried it to Eurystheus on his shoulder. The cowardly king hid himself inside a bronze urn when he saw Hercules marching up with the boar.

The Augean Stables

King Augeas was said to have the largest stable in all of Greece. It housed the divine cattle sacred to Helios, Augeas' father. It had not been washed in many decades. Moreover, the cattle were "divine" which meant they excreted thrice as much as normal cattle do. And the faeces were poisonous. Eurystheus wanted to humiliate Hercules and asked him to clean the Augean stables in a day. Hercules went straight up to the king and said he was going to clean the stables in a day. "I'll give you ten percent of the cattle if you do it!" challenged Augeas. Hercules went uphill and turned the courses of the two rivers Alpheus and Peneus to wash the stables. He collected his bounty and left in pride.

The Stymphalian Birds

These were the pet birds of Artemis. They had feathers of iron which they could shoot at their enemies. Their beaks were long and of bronze. Their excreta was extremely poisonous. They were destroying the crops and vegetation of Arcadia. Hercules could not capture them as they were pretty fast. The goddess Athena saw this and gave him a rattle. He shook the rattle and the birds flew away scared. Then he shot some of them with his arrows dipped in the hydra's blood. The rest of them flew away, never to return again. He brought some of the fallen birds to Eurystheus.

The Cretan Bull

This was the bull Pasiphaë (Minos' wife) fell in love with. When Hercules reached Crete, Minos was more than happy to let him take the bull as it was wreaking havoc on his land. But Hercules had to capture it first. This he did by jumping onto the charging bull and subduing it with his huge arms. Then he loaded it onto a ship and brought it back to Eurystheus who could not keep it securely. The bull escaped and charged into Marathon.

The Mares of Thrace

These were a herd of man-eating horses. They were uncontrollable and also breathed fire. Breathing fire was a common feature with many of these mythological beasts.

These mares were the property of the hero Diomedes of Thrace. He was the son of the god Ares. The savage Diomedes fed his guests to his horses. Then they were tied with iron chains. Hercules loosed the chains first and fed Diomedes to the horses. They became tameable upon eating their master. He then tied them up, gagged them and brought them to Tiryns. Eurystheus was scared to death and dedicated them to Hera.

The Girdle of Hippolyta

Queen Hippolyta ruled over the Amazons[28], a race of warrior-women living in secrecy. She was a daughter of Ares, the god of war. Ares had gifted her a "war-belt" to wear her sword and dagger. Eurystheus wanted this girdle for his daughter Admete. The Amazons were ferocious fighters and Hera had already warned them against Hercules. This time the hero was accompanied by another - Theseus, the slayer of the Minotaur. A bloody war ensued when Theseus abducted Hippolyta. He gave the girdle to Hercules and married the queen in Athens. Theseus and Hippolyta had a son named Hippolytus. But of course, Theseus abandoned Hippolyta after a while and married Phaedra. But that is a story for another day.

The Cattle of Geryon

Geryon was a giant who lived in the Hesperides islands. He had three heads, six arms and six legs. His most prized possessions were his cattle. Hercules shot him in the forehead with his poison arrows and then clubbed him to death. Hera, foaming with rage, sent fleas that bit and scattered the cattle. It took Hercules a year to find all the cattle and herd them back to Tiryns. Eurystheus sacrificed them to Hera. The ten labours were complete.

Hercules said to his cousin, "By Zeus, I've completed the Ten Labours for my rightful throne! Yield cousin!"

"The throne is not yours as you have received help in two of the Labours. You got Iolaus' aid in killing the Hydra. Diverting rivers to clean the stables is cheating," said Eurystheus timidly.

"What do you mean, cousin? What else do you want?" roared Hercules, raising his club.

"You must complete two more Labours to claim the throne," said Eurystheus. "It is Hera's will," he added in fear. So Hercules went on to do two more Labours.

The Golden Apples of Hesperides

When Hera was wedded to Zeus, she received a branch of golden apples from the goddess Gaia. She planted it in her orchard and commanded the Hesperides to tend to these apples. The Hesperides were a group of nymphs, daughters of the Titan Atlas. They guarded the golden apples sacred to Hera. So this time, Hercules was going to steal from Hera herself! But the hero decided on a detour first - he paid a little visit to Prometheus[29] in Mt. Caucasus. Prometheus was hanging, chained to a huge ravine; eagles chewing on his liver. Hercules promised to release Prometheus if he told him the whereabouts of the Hesperides. Then he tricked Atlas into getting the apples for him while he held the Earth on his shoulders for a while. He kept his promise to Prometheus and delivered the apples to Eurystheus.

The Guardian of the Underworld

The last and most dangerous of all labours was to capture and bring back Cerberus, the three-headed hound of the underworld. This beast was Hades' pet and posted at the entrance to the Underworld preventing souls from leaving and the living from entering the Underworld. Hercules got the help of Athena and Hermes to enter the Underworld. He asked the permission of Hades, the god of the dead and ruler of the Underworld. Hades told him he could have the beast if Hercules could tame it without using any weapon. Hercules managed to tame Cerberus with his bare hands. He even rescued Theseus on his way out. Theseus had been chained alive in the Underworld because he had tried to abduct Persephone. Cerberus had never seen daylight. When Hercules chained him and brought him outside the dark realm, he had to drag Cerberus. The infernal hound vomited and a spray of poisonous aconites grew up where his vomit fell. Hercules released Prometheus as promised and paraded Cerberus through Greece. He returned Cerberus to Hades after Eurystheus had seen the beast.

CHAPTER TWENTY-SIX

DEIANEIRA AND THE SHIRT OF NESSUS

"... His poisoned shirt
Still wet with blood he gave to Deianira,
Told her that all who wear it are possessed,
Seized by the magic of reviving love." Ovid,
Metamorphoses Book IX [233]

If you recall the story of Meleager, then you will remember that Deianeira was his half-sister. Deianeira was the daughter of Althaea and Oeneus, the King of Calydon. She was a ferocious woman - not your average princess. Deianeira was famous for driving her chariot and fighting from it. She was spotted by two men – Achelous and Hercules. Before we go any further, the name Deianeira translates as "husband-killer" - so it was with her tale. Now why would anyone want to marry a woman named "husband-killer"? It's like a bumper sticker announcing an accident. Nevertheless, Achelous and Hercules did not give up the princess. Achelous was in love but Hercules was after her kingdom. He wanted to expand his territory and annex Calydon to Tiryns.

Achelous was a powerful river-god who shape-shifted and morphed into water. Deianeira hated him and hoped her father would not give her in marriage to Achelous. But Hercules interfered and agreed to fight Achelous to get Deianeira. During the combat, Achelous shape-shifted into a serpent and a bull. Hercules broke one of his horns and defeated him. The horn was gifted to Ceres, goddess of agriculture who made it her cornucopia (also called the horn of plenty, the cornucopia was always filled with grains, vegetables, fruits and bread). Hercules married Deianeira and took her to Tiryns. They had to cross a flooded river on the way. A centaur named Nessus offered assistance. While Deianeira was attempting to cross the river, Nessus tried to rape her underwater. Hercules shot Nessus with his hydra-poison arrow. Nessus with his dying breath told Deianeira that his blood-stained shirt was a love potion. "The time will come for you to use my shirt to keep Hercules faithful to you," he warned her and died. She accepted his shirt and kept it away secretly. Little did she know that it was poison.

Hercules was known for his numerous affairs with various women. He fathered children all over Greece. The hero fell in love with Iole, the daughter of King Eurytus. Hercules abducted Iole and made her his mistress. Once again, Hera made him mad and he killed Iole. To receive his second purification, the Oracle of Delphi commanded him to be a slave to Queen Omphale for a year. Of course, you can guess what happened next.

Omphale was the queen of Lydia. She was the daughter of King Iardanus who died in a hunting accident. She ruled Lydia after his death. Now you have to understand that Omphale was an Asian queen. She was considered savage by the Greeks. In fact, the Greeks considered all non-Greeks as savages. Remember Medea? She was called 'savage' by her husband Jason. To serve an Asian queen was the most degrading punishment of all. To top it up, Omphale made Hercules wear women's clothing. She wore his lion skin and carried his club. He had to hold the thread while Omphale was spinning. She fell in love with him and married him after his servitude. They had a son named Lamos.

When she heard rumours of Hercules with Iole and Omphale, Deianeira gave Nessus' shirt to Lichus, Hercules' servant. She asked Lichus to take it to her husband and help him wear it. When Hercules wore the shirt, it stuck to his skin and melted it. Then it pierced his bones, all the while killing him slowly. When he tried to strip the shirt, his flesh came with it. He screamed aloud and broke the pillars of his castle. Even his bone marrow melted and fell like water. He raised his voice to Mt. Olympus and cried "Saturnia[30]! Are you happy now! Feast your eyes upon my death! If you indeed have one iota of mercy for the man who subdued the Centaur, send me swift death! These hands have toiled for the girdle of the Amazons, snatched the horn of Achelous, killed the Boar and skinned the Lion. Yet I suffer and the coward Eurystheus is spared! Are there people who believe that the gods exist?"

Maddened with pain, Hercules ran uphill Mt. Oeta. He uprooted pines and cypresses in his unbearable pain. Poor Lichus was terrified. Hercules flung Lichus off his castle into the sea. Lichus turned into a rock. Hercules made his own pyre with the trees he had uprooted and asked Philoctetes to light them up. Philoctetes was his best friend. Hercules gave his bow, quiver and hydra-poison arrows to Philoctetes who later shot Paris[31] with them in the Trojan War[32]. He spread the Nemean Lion's skin over the flames like a blanket and laid down over it - his last repose. The Olympian gods looked down and were afraid that the Earth would be unguarded if such a hero died. "I'm happy to announce that I'm going to make Hercules immortal. He has earned his place amongst us. If anyone objects, let them know that it is my right and my will to grant immortality," said Zeus. His warning to Hera made her quiet.

The funeral fire melted away Hercules' mortal features. Then he stepped up, magnificent and glowing with the light of Zeus. He ascended to Mt. Olympus. Zeus gave him ambrosia and made him a god. He also gave Hebe, the goddess of youth, in marriage to Hercules. She was the daughter of Zeus and the divine cupbearer to the gods. She was the most beautiful and the most respected because she kept the gods and goddesses young by offering them ambrosia. It is a bit surprising that the Norse goddess Idun did the same with her golden apples of eternal youth.

CHAPTER TWENTY-SEVEN

ORPHEUS AND EURYDICE

"And as they neared the surface of the Earth,
The poet, fearful that she'd lost her way,
Glanced backward with a look that spoke his love -
Then saw her gliding into deeper darkness,
And as he reached out to hold her, she was gone;" Ovid,
Metamorphoses Book X [261]

Orpheus was the divine minstrel of Thrace. He was the son of Apollo, the god of music, poetry and medicine, and Calliope, the Muse[33] of the epic. Apollo gave him a golden lyre and taught him to play it. Calliope taught him the art of making and singing heroic ballads. His music had the ability to lift rocks, move rivers and subdue animals. Hence, he was a divine bard. If you recall the tale of Jason, Orpheus was one of the Argonauts who went in search of the Golden Fleece. On the return voyage, the Argonauts had to pass through the island of the Sirens. It was Oprheus who sang sweeter than them and made them jump back into the ocean.

It so happened that Orpheus fell in love with Eurydice, a Naiad[34] of the forests. But Eurydice was already sought by another - Aristaeus, the bee-keeper. But Eurydice loved Orpheus and the wedding was fixed by Hymen. On her wedding day, Aristaeus tried to kidnap and rape Eurydice. She ran to escape her pursuer and was bitten by a venomous snake in the grass. Poor Eurydice died on her wedding day. Orpheus stood waiting and when Eurydice's corpse was borne down the altar, he burst into tears. But he was determined. He made up his mind to travel to the Underworld and beg Hades to give Eurydice back to him.

Orpheus reached Lake Avernus, the entrance to the Underworld armed with his lyre. Cerberus was guarding the gates but Orpheus played his music and Cerberus fell asleep. He went and stood among the shades[35] waiting for Charon's[36] boat. The Ferryman of the Dead refused to allow Orpheus on board because he was still alive. Orpheus played his lyre and Charon took him straight to the castle of Hades. The grim god was shocked to find Orpheus alive and breathing in the Underworld. "O king and queen of the dead! I'm not a person gifted with flattery. I have not come to stare at your dark kingdoms. I have come to collect the soul of my beloved Eurydice. However much I tried to accept her loss, Cupid's power over me is stronger. The very same Cupid joined you in love. So I know you can understand my feelings for her. Please, I beg of you, please unspin the fatal thread that was cut away or let me join my bride in her darkness," sang Orpheus. His tragic song made the shades weep. The Furies stood weeping and all the demons stopped their tortures for a while. Queen Persephone was in tears. She nodded towards her husband.

"We give you your Eurydice, divine singer. But on one condition, you must not turn back and look at her till you reach Lake Avernus. She will follow you but this you must do," warned Hades. He called for Eurydice and she came, pale and limping from her wound. Orpheus turned away and started playing his lyre. He slowly walked towards the entrance and he was extremely happy because he could hear Eurydice's faint footsteps behind him. After a while, the footsteps stopped. Afraid that she had lost her way, he turned back to look. And that was all. He caught just a glimpse of her gliding back into the shadows like smoke. One moment she was there. And then she was gone. He heard a faint "goodbye" but that could have been his imagination.

Eurydice was twice dead and lost to Orpheus forever. He wanted to go back to the Underworld but it was closed to him. He had lost his one chance. Orpheus became mad with melancholy. He was in rags and refused to eat or drink for a week. Later when his mood was better, he went back to Thrace. He refused the company of women because he feared he had bad luck in marriage and he could not think of marrying anyone else but Eurydice. But women followed him and felt insulted when he refused them.

Roaming the hills and valleys, Orpheus would sing from dawn till dusk. His songs were so sad they drew out all the plants. Every plant pulled out its root and walked towards him to listen. The rivers changed their courses. Birds and animals gathered around him and wept. He worshipped Apollo and no other god. A group of maenads passed by singing the praises of Bacchus. They threw sticks and stones at him taunting his music and calling him out to their rites. He refused to drink and partake in their merrymaking. In a frenzy, they tore him to pieces and threw them into the River Hebrus. His head was still singing. His lyre ascended to heaven where the Muses made it a constellation. He was buried on the island of Lesbos. Finally, he was reunited with Eurydice in the Underworld.

CHAPTER TWENTY-EIGHT

THE HYACINTH

"As in a garden, if one breaks a flower,
Crisp violet or poppy or straight lily
Erect with yellow stamens pointed high,
The flower wilts, head toppled into earth,
So bent the dying face of Hyacinthus," Ovid,
Metamorphoses Book X [266]

All of Apollo's friends and lovers had tragic violent deaths. Either that or they were transformed into trees or animals. Remember the sunflower? The frankincense? The laurel? This is a similar tale.

Apollo became so fascinated with a young boy named Hyacinthus. Some of these Greek gods and heroes were bisexual. Classical texts as old as Ovid's *Metamorphoses* throw light on homosexuality, bisexuality, transformed identities and transgenders. Coming back to Apollo; he dearly loved Hyacinthus and left his shrine at Delphi to accompany the boy in his hunting expeditions. They caught birds and set snares together. They played discus in the afternoon. On one such afternoon, Apollo threw the discus too hard. It shot up like a fire and vanished into thin air. Hyacinthus ran to retrieve it. But the fatal discus ricocheted off a rock and hit him full in the face. He fell flat and died on the spot.

The god of the sun grew pale and rushed towards Hyacinthus. He applied various herbs, potions and tinctures but life ran out of the boy. It was too late. Apollo took the boy in his arms and wailed, "O my poor child, you should have lived forever in my sight. But I am your murderer now. Your name shall forever echo from my lyre and be printed on the leaves of soft flowers." As he spoke this, Hyancinthus' blood froze in the grass below and from it, a tiny purple flower sprang up. Apollo scratched the name of Hyacinthus across its leaves. Thus this flower is called hyacinth from that day on. It was worn by Spartans to honour the memory of their sons lost in battle when they celebrated a feast on Hyacinthus Day.

CHAPTER TWENTY-NINE

THE SECRET WISH OF PYGMALION

"Pygmalion, after paying his devotions,
Began a prayer, then shyness overcame him;
He whispered, 'May the very Gods in Heaven
Give me a wife' - he could not say outright,
'Give me the girl I made.' Ovid, *Metamorphoses* Book X
[268]

There are many tales where the Creator fell in love with his creation. This is one such tale involving a man with a broken heart, a statue and a goddess. Pygmalion was the ruler of Cyprus, the island sacred to Aphrodite. Pygmalion saw something that made him hate women and take a vow of celibacy. What was it? Prostitution. It may be common now but Cyprus before the birth of Christ was shocked to witness beautiful women offering themselves in the streets. These women did not do it of their own free will. They were the daughters of King Propoetus who refused to construct an altar for Aphrodite. They did not worship "love" as they had plenty of other important work to do.

The goddess became angry and cursed them to "offer their own flesh against their will" and they became the very first prostitutes in Greece. Ovid comments that these women lost their ability to blush! They could not feel love either.

It was in this state that Pygmalion became celibate. He shut himself in his workshop and started sculpting. He made beautiful and life-like statues. One day, he sculpted an exquisite statue of a maiden. He poured his soul into his creation - as all passionate artists do. When he took the chisel off, the maiden stood in his workshop with extended arms towards him. He named her Galatea and you can guess what comes next. He fell in love with her.

Pygmalion bought her little trinkets every day. He gave her diamond rings for her slender fingers and pearls for her ears. He dared not touch her for fear of getting the statue dirty. He bought her everything maidens of her age loved - pet birds, semi-precious stones, sea shells, lilies of a thousand colours and amber. He dressed her like a princess and kissed her. He even took her to bed. If you think he's a pervert, you're wrong. Maybe right. What is love but perversion anyway?

Cyprus, being the domain of Aphrodite, hosted the Aphrodisia in the month of July. This was a Feast celebrated in honour of the goddess of beauty and love. The altars would be washed with the blood of a dove, the sacred bird of Aphrodite. Her images would be carried by maidens in love or married women. Young initiates offered salt (to commemorate Aphrodite's birth from the sea), bread, fire, incense and white flowers. There was merry-making and love was celebrated en masse. Pygmalion usually avoided Aphrodisia because his heart was broken but now he had a reason. He went to the altar of the goddess and gave his offerings. Then he prayed, "O foam-born goddess[37] of the fire burning in my heart, I pray to you. Please give me a wife..." he stammered and choked because he could not speak his heart "Give me the maid I made," he said. He was not aware that Aphrodite was standing in the crows disguised as an initiate. She heard his prayer. The altars shook and lamps flared thrice.

With great hope, Pygmalion came running home. He gently touched the statue. The cold ivory felt like melting wax. It was warm to his touch. He could feel her pulse. Slowly, Galatea opened her eyes and smiled at him. Aphrodite came down as the wedding guest and soon a daughter was born to them. She was named Paphos which is also the name of an ancient Greek city, supposedly the birthplace of Aphrodite.

CHAPTER THIRTY

CINYRAS AND MYRRHA

"He stroked her face and kissed his daughter lightly.
Then Myrrha brightened; when he asked her whom
She'd like to marry now, she whispered shyly,
'Some one like you.'" Ovid, *Metamorphoses* Book X
[271]

Cinyras was the son of Paphos and the grandson of Pygmalion. He ruled over Cyprus with justice. He was known for his physical beauty and charm. He was also known for creating many musical instruments and taught people the art of mining copper. Ovid says that he would have been a lucky man if he had been childless. But as fate would have it, he had a beautiful daughter named Myrrha. She was the cause of his destruction and death. Orpheus the divine musician sings this tale in Ovid's *Metamorphoses* and he advises fathers and daughters with troubled dispositions to leave the gathering as this tale would be a perversion. So if tales of incest and lust get you down, you should follow his advice and go over to the next chapter. This tale is included in this book because myths are like chained links - take out one and the meaning is lost. The origin of myrrh and the birth of Adonis cannot be skipped.

Moving on, Orpheus sings that a Fury from the darkest depths of Tartaros poured the venom of Styx upon Myrrha. Cinyras was a loving father. He brought suitors from all over Greece, the Arabian Gulf and India so his daughter could choose her husband. But Myrrha refused to even see them. Cinyras asked her, "I don't understand, Myrrha. These men are the best. Who would you like to marry?" She wept and told him, "Someone like you." Little did he know that Myrrha was actually in love with him, her own father. Poor Cinyras thought that Myrrha was afraid and needed more time. Meanwhile, Myrrha mused - "O gods in heaven, pity me! What exactly is right or wrong? Animals mate with their parents. Only our laws deny what Nature accepts. O how I wish he was possessed like me!"

Hopelessly in love, Myrrha decided to take her life. She was about to hang herself from the ceiling when her old nurse saw her. The poor old woman rushed forward and took the princess in her arms. She told her, "I think you're deeply in love. I will not tell your father." Myrrha grew angry and howled like a wounded animal. The nurse pressed her, "Who is it?" "My mother is so lucky!" Myrrha cried and the nurse understood everything. Her white hair stood on its ends. The nurse had an idea. She waited till the Feast of Ceres when Cinyras was busy honouring the goddess of agriculture. All women had to be pure during these rites and so they kept away from their husbands for nine days. Queen Cenchries, the wife of Cinyras, was the purest. The nurse went to Cinyras - who was drunk - and told him that a young maiden loved him. She said the maid was "as old as Myrrha". Cinyras asked the nurse to bring her to his chamber.

Myrrha was pleased for three nights. On the fourth, Cinyras lit a lamp and saw her. He went wild with horror. Myrrha ran away into the forests. Cinyras killed himself in fury. Myrrha wandered for nine months, pregnant and spent. She prayed for mercy and a nameless god (Ovid does not mention any deity's name - apparently no deity would show mercy for such a crime and even if he/she did, it was not honourable to name them) changed her into a tree. Lucina eased her labour and a boy was born from the trunk of this tree. The tree wept tears which later became myrrh. The dryads[38] washed him in his mother's tears and raised him. This was Adonis, handsome and charming - as cute as Eros himself.

CHAPTER THIRTY-ONE

APHRODITE AND ADONIS

"And on that day as Eros stooped to kiss her,
His quiver slipped, an arrow scratched her breast;
She thrust her son aside and shook her head
While that swift cut went deeper than she knew.
She found Adonis beautiful and mortal" Ovid,
Metamorphoses Book X [276]

Adonis, the charming son of Cinyras and Myrrha, great-grandson of Pygmalion grew up into the most handsome man in Greece. One day, when Eros (god of love) stood up to kiss his mother Aphrodite, his quiver slipped and a golden arrow pierced her breast. She saw Adonis wandering in the glades and fell in love with him. She abandoned her temples in Cyprus and Amathus. She followed him wherever he went. She saw him hunting wild animals and her heart throbbed. Aphrodite called her sweet Adonis and warned him to stay away from wild animals. "Your end will be the end of both of us," she said.

One day, Adonis went boar hunting in the forest. He did not listen to Aphrodite's warning, of course. The huge board stormed at him and stabbed him with its tusk. His blood flowed in rivulets and Cytherea[39] swiftly turned her swan-driven chariot towards him. She rushed to him but his life was already gone. She poured sweet nectar over his body and a pretty flower sprang up from his blood. This flower is called the anemone. It is a dainty flower and one touch will scatter all its petals.

CHAPTER THIRTY-TWO

Swift-Footed Atalanta

"As Hippomenes asked himself the question,
The girl flew past him as if feet were wings,
And to the boy from Helicon her speed
Was like a Scythian arrow's flight through air,
And she, of course, more beautiful than ever." Ovid,
Metamorphoses Book X [279]

Atalanta (this is not the Atalanta of the Calydonian boar-hunt) was a huntress dedicated to the cult of Artemis. She was a princess of Boeotia and had been abandoned at birth because her father wanted a son. She had vowed that she would never marry. The Oracle of Delphi gave her a confusing prophecy "Run from marriage, if not you'll lose everything that you are". Pleased with her hunting skills, Apollo gave her a gift - speed. She could run faster than the wind. Hence, she was known as the swift-footed huntress. But time passed and many young men approached the huntress.

"I'm not your kind. Know that you have to race me to win my hand. If you shall lose, however, death will be your gift," she said. That was a condition she had decided after meeting the oracle. Many left and few participated in the race. All were executed. One fine day, a young hero trained by the centaur Chiron approached her. "Why play with slow-footed fools? Come, play your race with me!" he said. This young man was Hippomenes, the son of King Megareus and a descendent of Poseidon. He was also one of the Argonauts who sought the Golden Fleece. Hippomenes was called 'the Undefeated' and he had a plan.

Atalanta had not cared for all those who went to their deaths before. This time, it was different. "Poor prince, I pray to the gods that he leaves the race. Let him escape a marriage that is poisoned with murder. Or rather, let him win," she mused. She had fallen in love with Hippomenes, the Undefeated. Hippomenes and Atalanta stood at the racing line. The young hero prayed to Aphrodite - "O Lady of Cypress, bless me with victory as you have inspired my love and I will build you a shrine," he prayed. Aphrodite heard him and gave him three golden apples from her sacred tree in the meadow of Tamasus. She told him how to use them. That was all he needed.

Horns blew and the race began. Atalanta flew past Hippomenes like an arrow. Her feet skimmed the road and she seemed to fly. Hippomenes knew he would have lost if not for the apples. He threw one apple far out so it landed right before the huntress. Its glittering light caught her eye and she stopped to pick it up. Hippomenes ran across her with the crowd cheering him. But half a second later, she outran him. He threw another apple; she stopped again but only for a brief moment. Hippomenes let her race on and threw the last apple when the finish tape was in sight.

Hippomenes ran past the tape and won! Atalanta lost but true to her word, married him.

Did Hippomenes keep his promise to Aphrodite? No. The goddess decided to take her revenge indirectly. Not long after the marriage, the young couple wandered into the forest towards an ancient temple. It was the shrine of Cybele[40]. There was a cave near the temple where ancient monks had left wooden statues of gods. Aphrodite increased their lust. Hippomenes and Atalanta had sex in the cave without any concern for the gods. Cybele was extremely angry and she transformed Hippomenes into a lion and Atalanta into a lioness.

CHAPTER THIRTY-THREE

THE WISH OF KING MIDAS

"So Midas said, 'Make everything I touch turn gold.'
Bacchus gave him the golden touch, yet thought
'What foolishness; it almost makes me sad.'" Ovid,
Metamorphoses Book XI [291]

Bacchus, the god of wine and revelry, wandered over Mt. Tmolus and reached the River Pactolus. He joined a group of drunk satyrs and nymphs in merry-making. There was a huge raucous. Bacchus noticed that his best friend Silenus was missing. In fact, Silenus was captured by Spartan peasants for drinking in their fields. They took him to Midas, King of Sparta. Midas dismissed the peasants and poured a round of drinks to Silenus. What a king! They drank together for ten days! On the eleventh day, Midas brought Silenus to Bacchus. The god was pleased to find his best friend in good health (and completely drunk). "Midas, my friend-in-drink, in return for bringing me my friend, I'll grant your wish. Ask and it is yours!" said Bacchus. Midas could have asked for a castle, a woman or a treasury full of gold. But he was fated to turn good things bad. "Make everything I touch turn gold," he said.

Once he got the golden touch, Midas ran home in joy. "What a fool! He will surely repent his wish," thought Bacchus. Meanwhile, Midas danced and touched the trees. They turned to solid gold. He plucked a fruit- it became polished gold. He took a handful of wet clay; that too became gold. He took an apple and it turned gold - almost like the apple of Hesperides. He touched a sheaf of wheat and he held a sprig of golden grains. He dipped his hands in the river and lo! It turned to a moving stream of gold. Midas went home and touched his castle. He asked his servants to bring every piece of furniture and changed them all to gold. He did not leave the statues, pots, pans and even the trees in his orchard. Everything gave way to his fancy. Tired, he sat down to a royal banquet laid out in gold. He broke the bread and found that it was a piece of gold. He took his goblet and drank his mouth was filled with cold, tasteless, liquid gold that he spat out. He bit into the meat and could not bite down further. It was no use. He could not eat and drink!

A frenzy of terror struck Midas. He raised his arms to Heaven and prayed to Bacchus. "O Bacchus, I accept my foolishness. What I asked was wrong. Take away your gift of gold - it's damned," he wept. Bacchus took pity on him and asked him to bathe himself in the river of Sardis. Midas journeyed to the holy river and dived in. He washed away his greed and gave his wealth to charity. He took to the forests and worshipped Pan. But that is not all. Midas simply couldn't keep his mouth shut. So he suffered.

Many years later, the playful god Pan came to Tmolus playing his reed pipe in full vigour. Apollo happened to be nearby and he heard the tunes. 'Who is that, playing so beautifully? Surely, he can't be better than me on my lyre' thought Apollo as he saw Pan. They entered into a fierce competition for which Tmolus himself agreed to be the judge. The mountain king came down from his abode to judge the music competition. Pan piped his rustic airs while Apollo took out his ivory lyre flashing with diamonds and poised his plectrum on his right hand (the lyre was supposedly the ancestor of the modern guitar). Tmolus listened and told Pan to throw his pipes away. The lyre won. Who could stand up to a rock concert anyway? Midas was among the audience and raised his voice to support Pan. Out of anger, Apollo gave him ass ears. Midas had to go around wearing a turban to cover his ears!

CHAPTER THIRTY-FOUR

THE FOUNDING OF TROY

"A short time later the job was done, the fee unpaid;
The king denied he owed them anything:
Why should he pay them?" Ovid, *Metamorphoses* Book XI [294]

King Ilus was the founder of the city of Troy. He sailed across the Hellespont and landed at a point between Sigeim and Rhodes. He had won a wrestling match at Phrygia and the prize was a cow. But he did not sail because of the cow, nor the match. An oracle told him that he would find a beautiful city for his descendants exactly at the place where the cow sat down on its hind legs. He travelled and found the cow that he had let loose sitting near a sacred altar built for Zeus the thunderer. To add spice to the dish, a statue of Zeus fell from the sky and landed on the spot before him! He then decided - that was the place to build a city for his people. He called the city Ilium after his name and his people became the Trojans. He married Princess Eurydice (not the wife of Orpheus) and she gave birth to Laomedon, the prince who would construct the famous Wall of Troy.

King Laomedon was a powerful but greedy man. He was the father of many strong and capable children, two of them being very famous in myth - Tithonus and Podarces, later known as Priam. Tithonus was the guy who fell in love with Aurora and had to endure eternal ageing. Priam was the King of Troy when the Greeks attacked it under the command of Agamemnon[41], thereby causing the Trojan War. Coming back to Laomedon, the King was involved in constructing a huge wall surrounding the city. It would be impassable when constructed. But Laomedon had run out of gold and men to do the job. Apollo and Poseidon arrived in disguise and agreed to do the job for payment in gold. Once the wall was constructed, the greedy king said, "Why should I pay you? You are not men, but gods and you did nothing but use your powers, unlike my men who toiled in sweat and blood." The gods were very angry. Apollo sent a plague that killed half the population. Poseidon sent a sea monster to destroy the other half.

Laomedon asked for forgiveness but Poseidon demanded his daughter Hesione to be sacrificed to the beast (similar to Andromeda being sacrificed to Cetus). Hercules was just returning from his adventures with the Amazons and stopping by Troy. He agreed to rescue the princess if he got to keep her. Hercules wanted Laomedon's magic horses - the famed horses that could ascend to Mt. Olympus and run over water. Laomedon agreed, the hero rescued the damsel in distress but once again, the king didn't keep up his promise. Hercules snatched the princess and sailed away roaring that he would attack Troy.

After completing the Twelve Labours, Hercules led a siege on Troy (so the siege of Agamemnon is the second siege of Troy). He had eighteen ships that sailed under the command of his friend Telamon. Laomedon attacked the Armada before they even got to land. Telamon was the first to breach the Great Wall of Troy. Hercules killed Laomedon and all of his sons except Podarces. He told Hesione that he would spare the lives of those she chose. She chose Podarces. Hercules said that her brother must first be her slave and later he must be ransomed to gain his life. Hesione agreed and Podarces went into slavery. He served her and Hercules for many years. Then he was marched out to be sold. Hesione paid for him by offering her silk veil that was gifted to her by Aphrodite. Podarces was ransomed and later became King of Troy. He was known as Priam; from the Greek 'priamai' which meant 'to buy.'

THE MARRIAGE OF THETIS AND PELEUS

"Old Proteus said to Thetis, 'Now's the time,
O goddess of the waters, for your embrace
To make you mother of son whose fame outreaches
Even his father's glory; greater than all the arts
His father knows of war and chivalry
Shall this child know.'" Ovid, *Metamorphoses* Book XI
[294]

Thetis was the most beautiful of all the Nereids and she lived in her father's splendid castle under the sea. She was dressed all in white and her long flowing tresses were adorned with branches of precious red coral. Her ivory neck was adorned with pearl necklaces and scallop shells. Both Zeus and Poseidon fell in love with her. As did many other gods, demigods and mortal men. But Thetis had a curse - her son would rival his father and if it were a god, then his godhead would fall forever. This prophecy was made by Themis, the goddess of divine law. "Greater than all the arts his father knows of war and chivalry shall this child know; far greater would be his victories, empires will fall beneath his feet," she had said. So that was why the mighty thunderer left her alone.

It was Peleus, son of Aeacus and grandson of Zeus, who fell in love with Thetis and did not care about the curse. Aeacus was the King of Aegina and known for his just rule. In fact, after his death, Hades made Aeacus one of the three judges of the Underworld. Peleus was born to this noble king and an Oread (a mountain nymph) named Endeis. His brother was Telamon (father of Ajax, one of the heroes of the Trojan War). If you recall the Argonauts, Peleus and Telamon were among Jason's company. They had also laid siege to Troy with Hercules. It was a bitter fate that Peleus' son had to die in the second siege of Troy.

Now Peleus was not that innocent. He was a murderer and married before he set eyes on Thetis. Peleus and Telamon failed to rescue their half-brother Phocus, son of Aeacus and Psamanthe, from a sea wolf. Psamanthe was a Nereid and also Thetis' sister, so this whole thing sounds weird. Anyway, according to Greek law, Peleus had to be purified by a King because he failed to protect his kin. So he went to Phthia where King Eurytion purified him. He also married Eurytion's daughter Antigone. They had a daughter named Polydora. Then Peleus killed Eurytion during the Calydonian Boar hunt and had to be purified by King Acastus. Astydameia, Acastus' wife fell in love with Peleus and when he didn't respond, she spread the rumour that Peleus had raped her. Acastus tried to kill Peleus but Hermes rescued him. Antigone hanged herself when she received news from Astydameia. The evil queen had sent her a message that Peleus was about to marry Acastus' daughter. In the end, Peleus killed both Acastus and Astydameia.

Thetis often came to the shores of Thessaly and basked in the sun. She went to a cave, half-hidden with overhanging creepers and berries. She drove her dolphin chariot to the cave and spent her day eating berries and sleeping upon the soft seaweed. Peleus watched her and seized her when she went to sleep. He tried to rape her but she was a master shape-shifter. Thetis changed into a tree, a bird and a leopard all at once. Peleus could not control her and let her go. He sat down in deep thought and prayed to the sea gods, who never let prayers go unanswered. He offered a goblet of wine as libation, lit a fire on the beach and threw a lamb into it. Then he saw Proteus, the Old Man of the Sea and the herder of the sea beasts, rise up from the waves. "O son of Aeacus, make a net and bind Thetis. She will then yield to you," he said.

The next evening, Peleus waited till Thetis came to her cave and went to sleep. He had already made his trap, a firm but gentle net. He seized her again and bound her in the net. Thetis could not shape-shift once she was bound. She yielded and agreed to be his wife (actually he forces himself upon her and she has no choice; these poets always sugarcoat tales of rape and incest).

Nereid and Doris held a splendid wedding feast for Thetis and Peleus. All the gods and goddesses were invited to the feast. Homer records that Zeus offered an immortal suit of armour as a wedding gift. Poseidon gave a pair of immortal horses. Athena brought a spear with a special bronze tip made by Hepahestos. But the goddess Eris was left out - no one invited her (who would want chaos and confusion in their wedding, eh?). So Eris marched in, grim-faced and said, "I too have a gift" - much like the evil witch in "Sleeping Beauty".

The guests were getting ready for "apple-throwing" where ripe apples would be thrown at the couple. It was a fertility ritual where Hera would bless the couple with children. Eris threw a golden apple - the Apple of Discord - that she had taken from Hera's garden protected by the Hesperides. The "apple-throwing" stopped and the goddesses had their eyes on the wondrous golden apple, glittering among the dull red earthy ones. "To the fairest, does this apple belong," said Eris. Hera, Athena and Aphrodite wanted the apple. They started fighting tooth and nail. Then they decided to go and ask Paris, son of King Priam of Troy, for his judgement. They vanished and the feast continued. In the years that passed, Thetis gave birth to seven sons. All died except one, the famed hero named Achilles.

Thetis lamented the death of her six sons. When the last one survived, she had a prophecy. It was in her son's fate that he would be either glorious but die young in battle or inglorious and live a long life. His death walked hand in hand with his victory. So she named him Achilles (Achos = lamentation and Kleos = victory in war). Peleus gave his son to Chiron the Centaur for training and upbringing. Homer and Ovid never mention Thetis dipping Achilles in the Styx to make him invincible. Achilles was a mortal like all other heroes before him - he was not blessed with the blood of the gods like Hercules. But Achilles grew up to be the best warrior in all of Greece.

CHAPTER THIRTY-SIX

THE JUDGEMENT OF PARIS

"She [Aphrodite] with a subtle smile in her mild eyes,
The herald of her triumph, drawing nigh
Half-whisper'd in his ear, 'I promise thee
The fairest and most loving wife in Greece.'" Tennyson,
Oenone https://www.poetryfoundation.org/poems/
45373/oenone

King Priam and Queen Hecuba of Troy ruled the land with peace and justice. If you go back to the tale of Hesione and the veil, you will recall Podarces/Priam being saved by his sister from Hercules. That's the guy who ruled Troy during the marriage of Peleus and Thetis. It's all connected, yeah. Priam and Hecuba had a bunch of kids - approximately 80 in total, many of them being killed during the second Trojan War. Some of these became great heroes in their time. Hector, the first son and Prince of Troy, was the best warrior in Asia. He was also the commander of the Trojan army. Paris, Hector's brother, was an expert archer, though depicted as a lover-boy in many sources. Some of the others were Troylus, Hippodamas, Melanippus, Polydorus, Cassandra, Laodice, Creusa, Iliona and Polyxena (these are notable heroes and they all have tales of their own).

Troylus was the famous prince of Troy who fell in love with Cressida, whose father had switched sides with the Greeks. Chaucer, Shakespeare and many other poets have composed the tragic tale in their verses. Cassandra was a princess of Troy who had the gift of prophecy. But she refused the advances of Apollo and was cursed that nobody would believe her. In fact, she predicted the whole war but no one listened to her. Creusa was married to Aeneas, the hero of Virgil's *Aeneid*. Creusa supposedly dies while Aeneas escapes with his sick father destined to find another land for the Trojans. Iliona was the first daughter of Priam and Polyxena was the youngest. Polyxena was sacrificed over the tomb of Achilles to appease his spirit and bring favourable winds for the Greeks to sail home.

Coming back to Paris, when Hecuba was pregnant with him, she dreamed that she gave birth to a flaming torch. Of course, this meant ruin - the city of Troy would be destroyed by the boy. The Priestess of Apollo arrived to ritually sacrifice the baby to save the kingdom. However, Priam tasked his huntsman to take the baby and kill it in the woods, far away from the palace. Yes, I know, this goes like "Snow White and the Huntsman." This is where you must understand that these myths are linked to every tale you have ever read. They are the structure upon which modern literature is built. And it is a sturdy structure indeed. The huntsman couldn't do it. He took the child home and reared him as his own. He took a dog's tongue to Priam and showed it as proof. Priam rested easy as his beloved Troy was safe. He was wrong.

Paris grew up to be very handsome and charming. He was not all cowardly as shown in the movie *Troy*. When he was a young boy, he confronted cattle thieves and restored the animals back to the shepherds. They called him Alexander which meant "Protector". He was famed for his judgement skills. He reared wild bulls and trained them to fight. Once he conducted a bullfight and called for shepherds to contest their bulls with his. The prize was a golden crown. The god Ares appeared in the form of a bull and defeated all of Paris' bulls. Paris gave Ares the crown without any thought. That was why the gods and goddesses came to him when they needed to be judged. Wonder why Hades didn't pick him to be a judge of the Underworld...he was perhaps too charming for the Underworld?

Hera, Athena and Aphrodite arrived at Mt. Ida, asking Paris to be the judge. He was supposed to choose "the fairest" among them. Hermes was the witness. The first thing that Paris did...ahem...was to ask them to undress. He wanted to see their 'beauty' to judge them. Evidently, Zeus allowed it, himself being amused. Even then, Paris could not choose as they were all equally beautiful. Then the bribing began. "Psst...I will make you king of vast kingdoms that stretch far like the sea...I will grant you untold riches," said Hera. "I will give you the strength of a hundred warriors and grant you all the wisdom of this world, the wisdom of the world beyond and even the wisdom of the unknown frontiers of death," said Athena. "Boy, I will give you the most beautiful woman on the earth," said Aphrodite. Of course, Paris chose Aphrodite. The 'beautiful woman' in question was Helen, wife of the formidable Menelaus. Oh boy, did she forget to tell him that Helen was already married. So Paris had to fight for his prize. And being married didn't mean anything serious those days either.

The abduction of Helen has entirely nothing to do with love. It was a planned political move. In fact, Menelaus knew this when he married Helen. During the 'bridegroom-choosing ceremony' conducted for Helen by her father Tyndareus of Sparta, all the suitors agreed to Odysseus'[42] plan. What was the plan? That they would help Helen's future husband retrieve her if she was abducted. They knew very well and even expected that Helen would be abducted because it had already happened in similar cases.

CHAPTER THIRTY-SEVEN

THE FACE THAT LAUNCHED A THOUSAND SHIPS

"He [Agamemnon] knew an angry virgin like Diana
Would need the solace of a young girl's blood.
When he began to feel that public duty
Was of more consequence than private virtue
(The politician overruled the father)
King Agamemnon, while her servants wept,
Took Iphigenia to a blood-stained altar" Ovid,
Metamorphoses Book XII [314]

So do you think you're beautiful? Every woman is a queen at heart. Every woman is beautiful in her own unique way. Helen was a problem. She is what W. B. Yeats called "terrible beauty." She was the daughter of Queen Leda, the wife of King Tyndareus of Sparta. Leda was the Greek equivalent of Snow White. She had pale skin and flowing locks of black hair, uncommon in Greek women. Zeus seduced her in the guise of a swan. In fact, the tale turns out to be similar to that of Alcmene. Leda became pregnant by Zeus and Tyndareus at the same time. But she laid two eggs like a bird. Helen and her sister Clytemnestra hatched from one egg. The twin brothers Castor and Pollux hatched from the other. But we do not know who the children of Zeus were. Helen was the most beautiful woman in the whole world, well, at least to what was known as the whole world at the time. And she caused a massive war that ruined a city and killed thousands of innocent people.

When Helen was quite young, she was abducted by Theseus (the guy who killed the Minotaur). Theseus left her with his mother Aethra in Athens and left. His friend desired to win the love of Persephone, the wife of Hades. Theseus helped him go to the Underworld but there Hades found out their plan and imprisoned them in Tartaros. In the meantime, Castor and Pollux waged war on Athens to rescue their sister. They not only saved her but also took Aethra as revenge! That is a tale for another day. Soon enough, Tyndareus called for a ceremony to choose a suitable husband for Helen. Many came, some of them kings, princes, demigods, warriors and heroes. Most famous among them were Odysseus, Diomedes, Ajax, Menelaus and Patroclus. Menelaus did not come but sent his elder brother Agamemnon in his stead. Agamemnon was a powerful war-mongering king ruling over Mycenae and nobody wanted to mess with him. Tyndareus did not want Agamemnon to capture his lands, so of course, he gave Helen to Menelaus. The others agreed to Odysseus' plan - that they would fight with Menelaus to retrieve Helen if she was abducted.

Menelaus and Helen had a daughter named Hermione when Paris visited Sparta. Agamemnon and his furious brother had occupied all of the islands near Asia Minor. Troy was the only city standing unconquered. Priam sent Hector and Paris to sign a peace treaty with Agamemnon and Menelaus. There was much dancing, feasting and revelry. And Paris abducted Helen while the others were getting drunk. Or she eloped with him. There is much confusion over this but going over Herodotus, Ovid, the poems of Sappho and the reunion of Helen and Menelaus presented in Homer's *Odyssey*, let's assume that she left of her own free will. Anyway, Helen left and Menelaus was furious. He ran over to Agamemnon who called all the suitors of Helen demanding that they fulfil their oath. They agreed and thus Helen became the beauty who 'launched a thousand ships and burnt the topless towers of Ilium' (the words of Christopher Marlowe). Agamemnon mustered the Mycenaean army and also the ships of all his colonies. But he could not get Achilles to join. And the siege would be futile if Achilles did not come.

Achilles and Agamemnon were at each other's throats because of Iphigeneia, the daughter of Agamemnon and Clytemnestra. Agamemnon had married Helen's sister and he was going to sacrifice Iphigeneia so that the siege would be victorious. What a dad! Agamemnon had a dream where Artemis appeared and demanded that his daughter be sacrificed if he wanted to conquer Troy. Iphigeneia, the daughter in question, was engaged to Achilles. So now you get the point. He fell out with Achilles who refused to fight for him. So Agamemnon sent Odysseus to get Achilles back into the team.

Since Thetis already knew Achilles' fate (he was either bound to die young but glorious or old but infamous), she sent him to live with King Lycomedes as soon as she heard about Agamemnon assembling an army. Achilles was disguised as a maiden and lived in the harem of the king under the name of Pyrrha. He raped Deidamia, daughter of Lycomedes, and she gave birth to a boy named Neoptolemus. When Odysseus saw the hero, he devised a plan and went back. Odysseus was known for his cunning wit and intelligent mind. He appeared as a peddler and displayed his wares outside the palace gates. He had brought two baskets - one with pearls, rubies, perfumes and cosmetics. He placed a sword in the other. The women rushed out to buy Orient pearls, silks, Arabian perfumes, incense, sandals and trinkets. Achilles took the sword and Odysseus caught him.

"O hero of heroes, Achilles, son of Peleus, what justice is there in dressing up courage to defend life? Why do you tarry under women's clothes? What honour is there in not facing your enemy?" spoke Odysseus. He was known for his honey-coated words.

"Hail, Odysseus! Nothing goes unnoticed by you, you wily snake. It's my mother, afraid for my life. I did this to give her peace," said Achilles. "Why must I fight for your commander when he has dishonoured me?"

"It's for your country you are fighting, Achilles. We are Greeks and we fight for her," said Odysseus.

"Ah, I'm sure Agamemnon is fighting for his own treasures. Well, I'm done. I have given him enough. He slaughtered my love and took my spoils of war. If you ask me, we must not go to war over a woman. Helen is one man's problem. Why kill so many souls over one man's ambition?" spoke Achilles in rage. He was known for his venomous rage.

"Come, come, Achilles. There are many reasons for war. But when she comes, we fight without questions. The whole of Greece has assembled. This war will go down in history as the greatest war of all - one where so many heroes fought and perished. If you fight and come back, you'll have songs of victory composed for you. You'll be given kingdoms, and queens with exceeding beauty and wealth beyond the world. If you die fighting, laments will be sung for you and you will be immortalised forever. You will have your glory. So what say you?" Odysseus said. He had prepared this speech beforehand, hinting on the 'glory' part because he knew that Achilles cared for nothing but ambition. He was right. Achilles wanted to be remembered forever as a hero. He had already made his mark among the Achaeans (Greeks) as the best warrior. And he was only in his teens - probably sixteen years old!

Poor Thetis was in tears. "I reared my son like a tree, with love I watered it, with love, I watched it grow day by day, hour by hour, till the woodcutter came..." she sang. It was a lament for his doom. Achilles took Patroclus, his 'squire', best friend and advisor with him. He wore the armour of Zeus, the one gifted to Peleus by the mighty thunderer. Achilles was also the commander of the Myrmidons, a group of formidable soldiers said to have descended from ants. They were loyal to a fault, stronger than any other Greek army and had their own ships. So, the entire Greek armada sailed to Troy, hoping to crush the rising city and plunder her riches in the name of revenge.

CHAPTER THIRTY-EIGHT

THE NINE-YEAR SIEGE

"Jove has sent us this sign, long in coming, and
long ere it be fulfilled, though its fame shall last for
ever.
As the serpent ate the eight fledglings and the sparrow
that
hatched them, which makes nine, so shall we fight nine
years at Troy, but in the tenth shall take the town.'"
Homer, *Iliad* [40]

Agamemnon's contingent was a massive one. He commanded not only the Greek forces but also those of his colonies in Asia. Thucydides records around 1200 ships in his *History of the Peloponnesian War*. Homer's *Iliad*, *Odyssey* and Ovid's *Metamorphoses* provide a huge catalogue of armies led by well-known heroes of the time. To be both brief and informative, this tale will include only the well-known heroes. Agamemnon led the whole force with his Mycenaean army. Ajax the Great (cousin of Achilles) led the warriors of Salamis, Menestheus led the Athenians,

Diomedes commanded the Argives, Menelaus the Spartans, Odysseus brought his troops from Ithaca and Achilles stood with his Myrmidons. Agamemnon brought a prophet named Calchas (Thestorides in Ovid's *Metamorphoses*) with him to predict the outcomes of the siege. Calchas was once a Trojan but he had joined the Greeks out of fear. The Trojans had their contingent as well, but much smaller. They were led by Hector, a formidable fighter and the first prince of Troy. Aeneas, the son of the goddess Aphrodite and Anchises, was the commander. Virgil hints that a small army of Amazons fought for Troy as well.

Before reaching Troy, the Greeks stopped at Aulis to pray for fair winds. They also wanted to return home safely. The Greeks beheld an amazing sight in Aulis. A serpent climbed on a tree and crept into a bird's nest. It devoured eight hatchlings and then the mother bird. Suddenly, the serpent turned into stone! Calchas prophesied that the Greeks would siege Troy for nine years and capture the city only in the tenth year.

When they landed in Troy, Calchas also predicted that whoever set foot on Troy first would die in the first battle. All were reluctant to jump out of their ships. Odysseus secretly threw his shield on the beach and jumped on it. Seeing this, Protesilaus leaped out. He was King of the Phylesceans and had been one of the suitors of Helen (remember Odysseus' agreement?) He fought bravely and was killed by Hector in the first wave of the siege outside the Trojan Wall. Thucydides in *The History of the Peloponnesian War* remarks that the siege was poorly planned. Many ships landed miles apart from each other. They scattered away to attach and pillage neighbouring islands after seeing the impassable Trojan War. Since they could not enter the city, they started farming the land and lost all their money. Ajax and Achilles went on campaigns of their own and reunited with the Greek contingent after eight years, doing nothing to fight the Trojans.

There was a prophecy that if Troilus lived to adulthood, Troy would remain unbreached. Troilus was a beautiful young prince of Troy, the son of Hecuba (Queen of Troy) and the god Apollo. Troilus was in love with Cressida, the daughter of Calchas. Though she loved him at first, later she changed her affections to Diomedes, the Greek commander of the Argives. Troilus was distraught and went out of the wall to fetch water. Achilles saw him and chased him into the temple of Apollo on the outskirts of Troy. Troilus hid under the altar but Achilles found him, dragged him by the hair and slaughtered him on the altar. Apollo was disgusted with such violence and decided to kill Achilles in the weakest manner possible. The Trojans found Troilus' corpse and wailed over his death. Priam knew there was nothing he could do to stop the Greeks.

Agamemnon and the Achaeans pillaged Apollo's temple after Achilles had killed Troilus. Chryse and his daughter Chryseis were the priest and priestess of Apollo. To make matters worse, Agamemnon took Chryseis as his concubine and also collected all the temple ornaments as his booty. Apollo was enraged and brought a plague upon the Greek army. In Book 1 of the *Iliad*, Chryses approaches Agamemnon requesting him to return Chryseis for ransom. Agamemnon refuses saying that the maiden was far more beautiful than his wife Clytemnestra. However, Achilles and Calchas order him to return her because the Greeks were dying by the dozens. Agamemnon returned the maiden but took Briseis, Achilles slave in return. This made Achilles angry and he refused to participate in the siege. He even wept to his mother (crying was not considered a sign of weakness in Greek mythology: Hercules, Odysseus and many others were often depicted crying) to make Zeus give victory to the Trojans so that the Greeks would realise the strength of Achilles! So if you observe carefully, Achilles remains inactive for most of the siege, nursing his anger and holding a grudge against the others.

There was another hero named Palamedes who was even more intelligent than Odysseus. Out of jealousy, Odysseus forged a letter that stated Palamedes received gold from Priam in return for poisoning Agamemnon. He placed this letter and Trojan gold from earlier booty in Palamedes' tent and alerted Agamemnon. When the letter was discovered, Agamemnon stoned Palamedes to death. Apollodorus in *Epitome* states that Nauplius, Palamedes' father, tried to get justice but he was refused. To get vengeance, he sent messengers to all the Greek queens to inform them that their husbands were returning with Trojan concubines. These concubines would soon dethrone the Greek queens. The Greek women were terrified and some of them took drastic measures. Clytemnestra (Agamemnon's wife) chose Aegisthus as her lover and planned to murder Agamemnon on his return.

After nine long years of confusion, disease, starvation, scarcity and suffering, the Greeks decided to abandon the siege. The goddess Athena walked down from Mt. Olympus and told Odysseus to persuade the warriors. Athena was a patroness of heroes and only these heroes could see her. Odysseus persuaded everyone aided by the speed of Athena and they decided to fight on. That was when they recalled the prophecy of Calchas. Troy would fall in the tenth year.

CHAPTER THIRTY-NINE

THE COMBAT FOR HELEN

"'If you would have me do battle with
Menelaus, bid the Trojans and Achaeans take their
seats,
while he and I fight in their midst for Helen and all her
wealth. Let him who shall be victorious and prove to be
the better man take the woman and all she has, to bear
them to his home, but let the rest swear to a solemn
covenant of peace whereby you Trojans shall stay here
in
Troy, while the others go home to Argos and the land
of
the Achaeans.'" Homer, *Iliad* [65]

The Trojans and Greek armies were assembled outside
the wall, ready to fight. They marched in silence and
strength, their feet raising the dust like a sandstorm.
Suddenly, Paris rushed out and announced that he would
take Menelaus in a single combat. "Why kill thousands
when one man's life can settle it all?" he said. "I accept. And

that one man shall be you!" stormed Menelaus. The others were relieved and they withdrew in joy. Agamemnon announced that the combat would begin with a royal sacrifice. Both armies brought a black ram and a white ewe. Their commanders made the sacrifice to Zeus and agreed on the terms. The victor was to receive Helen and her riches (the kingdom of Sparta). Hector was very worried because he knew his brother.

"Evil-hearted Paris, fair to see yet weak at heart, woman-mad and false of tongue, I wish that you had never been born. It is better to die in combat than live without honour. The Achaeans will mock at us when they see that you are strong in love but weak in courage. Why did you have to steal that woman wedded to a warrior and bring sorrow upon the land of your fathers?" spoke Hector.

"I accept your rebuke, brother. But I have my skills too. Bid the Greeks keep their word and if I win, let them sail away in peace, leaving our land alone." said Paris.

The combat was fixed. Hector and Paris marched to the front. Hector helped his brother get into his armour and wear his sword. Odysseus tossed pieces of parchment into a helmet and the lot of Paris flew out first. It was Paris' chance to throw the spear at Menelaus. He took his aim but the spear bounced off Menelaus' shield. Menelaus prayed to Zeus for revenge on his wife. He threw the spear with such force that it pierced through the shield and armour of Paris. Menelaus pulled out his sword and grabbed Paris by the hair. He dragged him but the helmet strap broke and Paris ran away. "What honour is this?" said Menelaus as he rushed towards the running Paris. But the gods were watching from Mt. Olympus. Aphrodite covered Paris in a dark cloud and took him to his palace. She left him in his chamber, safe and unhurt while the whole Greek army was looking for him. Priam, Helen and all of Troy witnessed Paris' cowardice that day. Helen regretted that she had left a true warrior for a man of false tongue, a trickster and a cowardly one at that.

Zeus, the mighty thunderer, called all the gods to a council on Mt. Olympus. Hera complained long and loud that Zeus was favouring the Trojans. So too did Aphrodite and Apollo. Hera hated them and favoured the Greeks. Athena assisted the Greeks. Following the word of Zeus, Athena made the Greeks arm themselves and fight the Trojans outright without any more single combats and skirmishes. In the battle that followed, Menelaus was wounded. Machaon, the Greek physician, tended to his wound. Diomed fought extremely well that day. He killed many Trojan heroes. He saw Aphrodite trying to rescue her son Aeneas. He hurled a bronze-tipped spear into her delicate wrist. The spear went through and she wailed in pain and fainted. The precious ichor[43], the immortal lifeblood of the gods, flowed through her veins and splashed on the earth. Iris[44], the goddess of the rainbow, arrived in her chariot and whisked the wounded Aphrodite away into the heavens. Diomed went so far as to attack Apollo. This angered the god and he sent Ares to kill him. Ares and Enyo[45] gave immense strength to Hector who fought like a god that day. On the other side, Athena armed herself in Zeus' armour; she took her aegis, her golden helmet with four plumes, and her flaming spear and stepped onto her chariot to chase Ares away. With her by his side, Diomed wounded Ares, the god of war himself! If you ask me, Diomed must have been the hero of *Iliad*.

CHAPTER FORTY

THE TROJAN WAR

"Then, when
he saw dawn breaking over beach and sea, he yoked his
horses to his chariot, and bound the body of Hector
behind it that he might drag it about. Thrice did he drag
it
round the tomb of the son of Menoetius, and then went
back into his tent, leaving the body on the ground full
length and with its face downwards." Homer, *Iliad*
[620]

As the war progressed, Ajax, Diomed, Odysseus and Menelaus laid waste to the beach of Troy and slew many valiant Trojans. Hector and his men withdrew in haste and the prince went to see his mother. Hecuba brought him a goblet of wine and said, "O noble son, give a drink offering to Zeus and then be refreshed." Hector declined to drink and replied, "Honoured mother, bring no wine lest I forget my strength. My hands are filthy with blood and I'm not fit to make an offering to Zeus. Pray that he keeps Diomed and Ajax away from our walls or it will be the end of us." Hector went to see his wife Andromache and his infant son

Scamandrius. He kissed his child and said to his wife, "It may be that you will have to work the loom in some Greek noblewoman's house or fetch water at a stern master's bidding. I pray that my son may become a better warrior than me. May he keep you safe and live to see this city flourish." But deep down he knew that it was not going to happen.

Hector and Paris went through the gates and assembled the soldiers. They killed many Greek warriors that day. Apollo and Minerva decided to let Hector fight single combat that day. The lot was cast and Ajax was chosen as the Greek champion. They fought till night and the herald stopped them. It was customary not to fight at night. Hector and Ajax appreciated each other and exchanged gifts. Hector gave Ajax a silver-studded sword. Ajax gave Hector a gold belt braided with royal purple silk. They agreed on a truce that there would not be any fighting until the dead were cremated. Both Trojans and Greeks collected their dead, washed off the blood and performed quick funerary rites. Zeus was extremely angry with the Olympians fuelling the war. He called them and announced, "Hereafter, you will not aid the mortal heroes in any way." However, he consented to Athena's request that they make suggestions to the heroes.

The next day, a furious war broke out and Hector proved extremely victorious. The Trojans managed to turn the Greeks back to their ships. Corpses were strewn everywhere. The Trojans made a war camp outside the city to keep the people safe. The Greeks dug a trench around their ships and constructed a temporary wall. Agamemnon could not sleep that night. Nestor advised him that they would not get Troy, much less return home alive, if Achilles stayed away. Agamemnon accepted his folly and said, "Sir, I was wrong. I own it. I will make amends and give Achilles great gifts. Briseis, I will return. I will give him tripods, iron cauldrons, gold, horses, skilled workwomen from Lesbos (an island) and load his ship with gold and bronze. If Zeus grants us the city of Troy, I will give him beautiful women. He can marry one of my daughters; the choice is his. I will give him fertile lands and kingdoms of his own." Ajax and Odysseus were chosen to take the message to Achilles. They went to Achilles' tent, at the far edge of the group. Achilles was outside playing his lyre. He rose up when he saw the messengers. He took them in and seated them on purple cushions. He offered them wine and meat. They gave libations to the gods and ate their fill.

Achilles heard Agamemnon's message and replied firmly, "Odysseus, noble son of Laertes, I will not give in to this cajoling. I will not be appeased by Agamemnon or any other Greek because they are thankless. I have laid down my life for them yet I have nothing. And he took away the only woman I ever loved, slave though she may be. Menelaus has come so far for Helen. I too feel the same for Briseis. Agamemnon has good heroes like you, Diomed and Ajax. He has accomplished much already. He has wronged me. I do not need his gold or his wealth. I already have more than enough cauldrons, tripods and divine horses. Let me remind him that it is my father's duty to find me a wife. I will marry her and rule my father's kingdom. If Poseidon wills, we will set out our ships tomorrow and row back home. And I warn you as you are my best friends. Leave Troy. There is nothing for you here. Go back to your families." Achilles was stubborn and did not listen to anyone. The messengers went back and delivered his message to Agamemnon.

The son of Atreus (Agamemnon) was so disturbed that he couldn't sleep that night. He was afraid that Hector might set their ships on fire while he was sleeping! He woke Odysseus and Diomed. He sent them as spies to Hector's camp to see what was going on. On the other side, Hector sent Dolon to spy on the Greeks. Odysseus and Diomed walked over the trench and spotted Dolon coming toward them. They hid under corpses and captured him. Dolon told them everything. They understood that the very best fighters were camped with Rhesus, the fiercest horseman. Odysseus and Diomed killed Dolon and took his armour. Then they marched towards Rhesus' camp and killed everyone. They also brought his best horses and weapons to the Greek camp. The next day, Diomed got very close to Hector and would have killed him if Apollo had not pulled him back. Cowardly Paris shot an arrow at Diomed's right foot and still the hero pushed on! Odysseus, Diomed, Nestor and the others got back heavily wounded.

Achilles, the so-called hero of the Trojan War, stood watching the battle from his tent. He sent Patroclus to Nestor's tent to find the whereabouts of the wounded. Nestor's pain came from the absence of Achilles than from any physical wound. He told Patroclus, "Noble Patroclus, why should Achilles care about us? So many of our brave warriors have died and so many lie wounded. Yet he has not joined to help his comrades. Peleus made his son promise that he would fight among the foremost and help his peers. He gave me charge of his son. Oh, I wish that you, Patroclus, fought in his armour! That some god gave you Achilles' valour to strike fear into the hearts of Trojans." Patroclus looked grave but took the words of old Nestor.

The war went on but neither side was victorious. The Trojans saw an eagle carry a snake over their heads. The snake (a symbol of Zeus, according to the Trojans) bit the bird and it dropped the venomous creature down. Some of the Trojans took this as an omen that they should fight the Greeks in their own camp. Hector was wise enough. He said, "I don't believe in these omens, whoever they may come from. There is only one omen - that a man must fight for his country." He fought on and sent the Greeks back to their ships. But Hector was not ready to go back. He started fighting them in their ships. The Greeks made a living fence holding their swords and spears. Idomeneus, leader of the Cretans and lawgiver, provided weapons to everyone. The Greeks made a shield wall behind which their archers shot volleys of arrows. Agamemnon sounded a retreat and advised the Greeks to draw down their ships and sail away. Diomed and Odysseus inspired the warriors to fight on.

Hera saw the whole battle and she became furious. She had a plan. She dressed herself in a glittering robe made by Athena. She anointed herself with ambrosial oils and went to Sleep's cave. She bribed Sleep with a footstool made by Vulcan in return for making Zeus fall asleep. Then she took Sleep to Mt. Ida where Zeus was wreaking havoc on the Greeks. She enamoured Zeus to sleep with her while the Greeks won. The plan worked but not for long. The Trojans pushed them through the trench they had constructed near their ships. Ajax turned back and faced the Trojans while the rest of the Greeks retreated. Ajax stood on a boulder and received all the arrows while the others ran to safety. Patroclus saw this and went to Achilles. He wept and requested Achilles to grant him permission to fight. Achilles said, "Save the Greeks if you must, Patroclus, and save the ships from being fired by the Trojans. When you have driven the Trojans away from the ships, come back.

Do not engage further as you are tempted by success. More importantly, do not fight Hector and rob me of my glory. Apollo protects the man and the god will kill you."

Hector and his men set fire to the Greek ships. Achilles called all the captains of his Myrmidon ships. There were fifty of them. He called all of them into his tent and offered wine libations to Zeus. He prayed that Patroclus would return safely after driving off the Trojans. Then Achilles took his divine armour (gifted by Zeus at the wedding of Peleus and Thetis) and put it on Patroclus. The sight of Patroclus and the Myrmidons infused fresh courage into the hearts of the Greeks. The Myrmidons killed thousands of Trojans and saved the ships. The sky rained blood all over Troy as Patroclus killed Sarpedon, a son of Zeus and a friend of Hector. Patroclus took the Greeks as far as the Wall of Troy. Apollo warned him, "Draw back, Patroclus, for it is not your destiny to sack the city of Troy, nor is it that of Achilles who is far better than you." But Patroclus kept on fighting and suddenly, his helmet and armour fell away undid by Apollo. He had worn the armour of Achilles but now it failed him. Euphorbus (a Trojan) threw his shield that pierced Patroclus between the shoulders. Hector stabbed him with his sword and Patroclus died. Remember that it was Achilles who gave his divine armour to Patroclus. And Hector knew well that he was killing Patroclus. The Greeks also knew that they were being led by Patroclus. With his dying breath, Patroclus prophesied that Hector would die by the hand of Achilles and his death was very close.

Menelaus and Agamemnon tried to rescue the body of Patroclus but Hector chased them off. Hector took Patroclus' armour and weapons as his trophies (it was customary for the victor to take valuables from the slain as trophies). Ajax leaped over the body of Patroclus and covered it with his shield. He stood guard over the body while Hector drove away in his chariot. Glaucus (a Trojan) rebuked Hector, "Hector, you fight well but you left Sarpedon's body to the Greeks. We must now take Patroclus' body and exchange it with Sarpedon's." Hector was not going to give up such a prize. He took off his armour and wore Achilles' divine armour. Zeus was not happy. Hector cried aloud, "Hear me, Trojans and allies! I will give one-half of the spoils I took today from the Greeks to whoever kills Ajax and brings me Patroclus' body!"

The Trojans, with Hector at their head, charged around Ajax and Menelaus like wild wolves. Menelaus, with great difficulty, lifted the body while the Trojans were firing arrows at him. Achilles knew that Patroclus was dead because Thetis had told him so. When messengers came to his tent, he was furious. He kept saying, "I told him not to fight near Hector." Achilles threw sand over his head and beat his chest. He wailed so loud that Thetis heard him from the sea. She came jumping out of a sea mist and comforted her son. He took an oath in front of Thetis, "for it is by my hand that Hector will fall." Thetis said, "Then your death awaits you soon after that of Hector." She cried for the upcoming doom of Achilles. When she saw that Achilles did not have armour, she went to Hephaestos, the smith of the gods. She begged him to make armour for her son. Meanwhile, Achilles saw the skirmish around Patroclus' body and leapt into battle without any armour. Athena shielded him with a golden glow and the Trojans were scared to death when they saw Achilles charging at them like a madman.

Achilles retrieved the body of Patroclus. He washed the body and laid it upon a bier. He anointed the body and dressed his comrade in white. Then he said, "O noble Patroclus, I promised your father that I will bring you back. Now I have broken that promise. I will not bury you till I have brought back your armour and Hector's head. I will also honour you with the bodies of twelve Trojan heroes." Thetis reached Hephaestos' abode, a bronze castle studded with stars. The craftsman was busy making twenty tripods with golden wheels. These were crafted with such cunning that they could go to the assembly of gods and return on their own. Charis[46], the wife of Hephaestos, received silver-footed Thetis with honour. Remember that Aphrodite is the wife of Hephaestos. Homer makes a deviation here. Hephaestos respected and loved Thetis because she had taken care of him when he was an infant. He called his golden handmaids (robots) to serve Thetis.

Hephaestos worked on twenty bellows to charge his furnace. He threw in blocks of copper, silver, bronze, tin and gold. When the armour was ready, he wrought on it figures of the earth, the heavens, the sun, the Pleiades, the Hyads, Orion and the Bear, fair cities and wedding ceremonies. He also made a huge shield and chiselled a pastoral scene, a vineyard, cattle and lions. The outer rim was of the water of mighty Oceanus. The breastplate gleamed like fire. Finally, the helmet was completed and it had a golden plume flowing from the top. When Thetis brought the armour to Achilles, the Myrmidons were scared to look at it. Thetis preserved the body of Patroclus with ambrosia and nectar so it would remain intact till burial. Achilles rallied the troops and went back to Agamemnon who was pleased to have him back. Achilles wanted to fight right away (without breakfast) but Agamemnon called for a huge feast. They sacrificed a boar to Zeus and Agamemnon gave rich gifts to Achilles. He also gave Briseis back to him. Achilles, however, did not eat a morsel of Agamemnon's feast. He gnashed his teeth, his eyes gleamed like fire and he fed upon his own grief.

Achilles put on Hephaestos' armour and took his father's spear. This spear was forged with ash from Mt. Pelion and infused with the blood of heroes. None of the Greeks could wield it except Achilles. He took his immortal horses (gifted by Poseidon to Peleus) and lashed them to his chariot. The sight of Achilles at the head of the Greek army froze many Trojans. He killed thousands that day and was still strong. River Xanthus (a river god) fought Achilles when he drove the Trojans around the river. The river hurled into a huge flood but Hephaestos used his fire to turn the river to smoke. The Trojan soldiers ran back inside their wall. Priam had ordered the gatekeepers to keep the gates open till all of the warriors made it inside. Hector came last. It was too late. He sent all his men to safety and faced Achilles all by himself. Priam wept as he saw Achilles bear down on Hector like a monster.

Hector got on his chariot and ran till he reached the river Scamander. Achilles chased him at the head of the Greek army. He cried aloud that no Greek was to fire an arrow or throw a spear at Hector. The man who killed Patroclus was his marked kill. Hector knew there was no way out. He turned back and said, "I will no longer fly you, son of Peleus. I will stay and fight you even if it means my death. Let us give each other pledges by our gods to give proper funerary rites for whoever dies in this fight. I will take your armour and return your body to the Greeks if I win. And you do the same for me if you win."

Achilles glared through his fiery helmet and said in anger, "Fool, there are no pledges between lions and lambs. There are no pledges between us - you will die and pay me with your life for my beloved comrade who you have killed." They fought for a while but Achilles ended Hector's life by hurling his spear at his neck. Hector fell down and Achilles said, "I have laid you low, you who believed you could get away after killing the comrade of Achilles and dared to be my peer in battle. Dogs and vultures will now devour your corpse." He pulled out his spear from Hector's neck. Hector, with his dying breath, implored him, "I pray you by your life and knees, and by your parents, do not abandon my body to dogs and vultures. Accept the rich gifts of gold and bronze that my father will bring out to you and send my body home so that the Trojans may cremate me."

But Achilles was beyond the point of mercy. He answered with bitterness, "Dog, talk not to me of gold or of parents. I will cut your flesh and eat it raw if that is what I want. I will not accept gold or bronze. Though Priam should offer your weight in gold, I will refuse it and lay your body to be fed by dogs and vultures." Finally, Hector said, "I know you had a heart of iron. Valiant though you are, Apollo and Paris will slay you soon." Hector choked and his soul flew down to the house of Hades (the Underworld). Achilles stripped Hector and took his armour. The Greeks crowded around his body admiring the strength of Hector. Then they stabbed the corpse with their spears for fun. But Achilles disrespected the body most of all. He pierced Hector's calf muscles with a length of ox-hide and tied the corpse to his chariot. Then he lashed his horses and drew the chariot to the Greek camp. Old Priam saw his handsome son's mutilated corpse dragged along and his heart gave out. Hecuba wailed aloud and led the Trojan women in lamentation. Andromache (Hector's wife) knew nothing and she was heating water so Hector could bathe when he returned. When she heard the wailing, she trembled and climbed up on the wall. The plight of Hector being dragged was more than she could bear. She pulled her crown and flung it on the floor. She flung her golden veil aside (Aphrodite had made this veil that was presented to her as a bridal gift by Hector). Then she wailed and said, "Woe is me, O Hector; woe indeed, that to be undone by the son of Peleus. This cruel man had killed my father and seven brothers in Thebes. Now, he has killed you too." The Trojan women lamented the death of Hector as Andromache burned away his clothes.

The Greek camp was none the happier. Achilles refused to wash himself and feast in Agamemnon's tent. He said, "I will not eat nor bathe before laying Patroclus on the flames." He laid out Hector's body in the sand beneath Patroclus' bier in an unseemly way. Then he went and wept by the sea. Patroclus' ghost came to him and hovered over his head. It said, "Achilles, you have forgotten my rites in your anger. I wander by the gates of Hades and the boatman will not take me aboard with the others because my body is unburied. Our fates are indeed cruel as you too will join me soon as you are about to be slain under the Trojan wall. I have one last wish, O Achilles, grant me this. Let our bones lie together in one single urn, the two-handled golden vase given to you by your mother." The spirit vanished as Achilles brooded over its words till dawn.

As soon as the sun rose, Agamemnon's men brought wood. Achilles laid out his comrade over the funeral pyre. The Myrmidons wore their armour and threw locks of their hair over Patroclus' body. Achilles cut off his yellow hair that his father had let grow for the river Spercheius. Peleus had prayed to the river that he would offer his son's hair with a great sacrifice ritual if Achilles returned home safely.

Now that was not going to happen; Achilles knew that, so he offered his hair to Patroclus. Achilles lit the fire and sacrificed many sheep and oxen around the pyre. He laid out jars of honey, pots of unguents (fragrant ointments), four horses and pet dogs. He also brought twelve noble Trojans who he had captured and slit their throats. He threw these twelve men into the fire as he had done the animals. He was full of bitterness and fury. All the while, Hector's body lay in the filth.

After the funeral, Achilles and the Myrmidons poured red wine over the dying flames. They took the whitened bones of Patroclus and covered it in two layers of animal fat. Then Achilles laid them in his mother's golden urn. They heaped sand over the bier and made a mound. Achilles announced the funeral games for Patroclus. He gave rich gifts to the winners of chariot races, speed running and boxing. After the funeral games, Achilles did another horrible thing. He lashed Hector's body to his chariot and drove it thrice around the tomb of Patroclus. Zeus saw everything from his throne and summoned Thetis. She rose up from the sea and went to Mt. Olympus. Zeus offered her a golden cup and gave her sweet ambrosia. Then he said, "For all your sorrow, you have still come out to hear me. For the past nine days, your son has desecrated the corpse of Hector. Now Hermes would steal it, but out of our mutual respect, I ask you this. Go to your son and ask him to accept Priam's ransom. Let him return the body as all the gods are angry about this." Thetis came down from Mt. Olympus and told her son everything. Achilles accepted as it was the will of Zeus.

King Priam, broken at heart though he was, took a large ransom to claim Hector's body. He went alone to the Greek camp and found Achilles in his tent. He went down on his knees and kissed the hands that had killed so many of his sons. Priam said, "O Achilles, think of your father, who is like me of old age. He is a happy man for he has you. Yet I have lost all of my sons. The bravest of Hector, for who I have brought you rich ransom. Fear, O Achilles, the wrath of Heaven and have compassion on me who has raised my lips to the hand of him who slew my son." Achilles started weeping as he would never see his father again. Priam went for Hector. Achilles raised Priam up and said, "Unhappy man, you have indeed been courageous. I care not for the gods as they mix up evil into the hearts of those who do good. My father Peleus was endowed with everything from riches to an immortal bride, yet he was blessed with only one son who would die far away from him. You too, Priam, were happy before all this. I give up Hector's body as it is the will of Zeus."

Achilles accepted the ransom and called his servants to wash the body first. He took the body far away as it may cause Priam to weep even more if he saw his mutilated body. Achilles wrapped the body in silk shirts after anointing it and placed it on Priam's cart. Then he sacrificed a sheep and prepared supper for Priam. He brought bread and wine. After supper, Achilles and his servants spread good rugs and prepared a bed for Priam. As Priam went to sleep, Achilles said he would delay the war for twelve days to bury Hector and conduct funeral games for him. But Priam did not sleep that night for fear that Achilles might change his mind. So he lashed his horses and brought the body inside the Trojan Wall before dawn. The noblewomen of Troy placed the body in Priam's palace and surrounded it with minstrels singing songs of lament. Andromache, Helen and Hecuba led the lament. Helen wept because Hector had always been kind to her like a brother.

The Trojans lamented their hero for nine days and brought wood on the tenth. They raised a bier and placed the body on it. They lit a fire that burnt all day. On the eleventh day, they quenched the fire with wine. Priam and his kin gathered the bones of Hector, covered them in soft purple robes and laid them in a golden urn. They placed the urn in a grave and covered it with large stones. Then they built a barrow over it and heaped sand over it to make a mound. Then they held a high feast in the house of Priam and celebrated the funeral with games. Homer's *Iliad* ends with the funeral of Hector. Surprisingly, nothing is mentioned of the Trojan horse or the death of Achilles. The tale continues in Virgil's *Aeneid* and Homer's *Odyssey*.

CHAPTER FORTY-ONE

THE DEATH OF ACHILLES

"He guided Paris' bow in that direction,
Then drew the arrow with his fatal hand.
At last - it was the first breath of true pleasure
Old Priam knew since Hector fell to death.
Then great Achilles who outfought the bravest,
Had fallen prey to one whose best performance,
Timid at the best, was stealing wives of Greeks!" Ovid,
Metamorphoses Book XII [332]

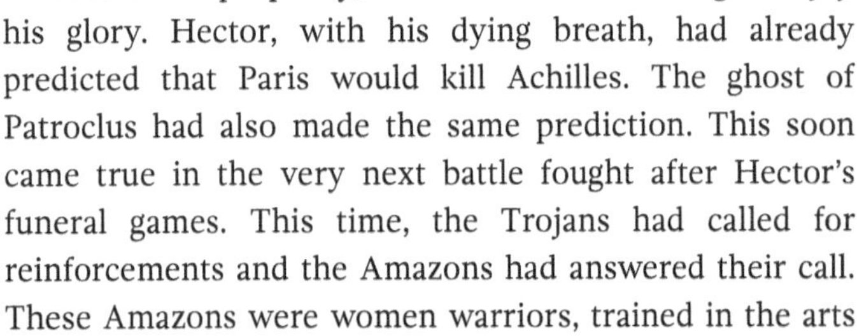

True to the prophecy, Achilles did not live long to enjoy his glory. Hector, with his dying breath, had already predicted that Paris would kill Achilles. The ghost of Patroclus had also made the same prediction. This soon came true in the very next battle fought after Hector's funeral games. This time, the Trojans had called for reinforcements and the Amazons had answered their call. These Amazons were women warriors, trained in the arts of battle from childhood. Priam hoped that Queen Penthesileia, ruler of the Amazons, would cut off the

Greeks and send them home.

Penthesilea was the daughter of Ares and a mighty warrior, so strong that she fought Achilles and gave him a tough fight. Arctinus Milesius' *Aethiopis*[47] depicts Achilles falling in love with Penthesilea moments before killing her. But Achilles accepted that she could have rivalled him in swordsmanship. Achilles ruthlessly killed many Trojans - soldiers and civilians alike - before Apollo alighted on the battlefield. The god of the gleaming bow beckoned Paris and told him to shoot an arrow at Achilles. The son of Peleus, in all his ruthlessness, failed to notice Paris aiming his bow at him. Apollo touched the arrow and guided it stealthily to pierce the armour of Achilles. The hero of the Trojan War fell beneath the Scaean Gates just as predicted by Hector.

Ovid laments the fall of the greatest warrior at the hands of a womaniser and a coward at that! Death by the hands of axe-swinging Amazons would have been honourable. The son of Peleus ended up in his mother's golden urn - a half handful of ashes. But his name lives on and in his name, all weapons go to war. But Achilles did not have a good afterlife (how could he go to Elysium after all the murders in the name of war?) Homer's *Odyssey* shows Achilles as a thirsty ghost in the Underworld. Odysseus hailed Achilles as a blessed soul but the ghost sadly replied that he would rather be a slave on Earth than a king of the dead. Dante places Achilles in the second circle of Hell in his *Inferno*. Achilles and a host of other fiery-tempered ghosts are swirled around in an infernal hurricane for their uncontrollable passions.

Achilles' funeral was celebrated with games and feasts led by Agamemnon and Menelaus. But there arose a dispute soon enough - who should beget the divine armour of

Achilles? Remember that Achilles' armour was made by Hephaestos, the smith of the gods. Armour was valuable property in those days of war and divine armour was even more special. The dispute was brought on by Ajax and Odysseus. Agamemnon called for a debate where both presented their claims. Ajax was first. He lifted his seven-tiered shield and glared at the Greek warriors seated on the beach. Then he said, "It's easier to talk, to tell a lie, than fight. I'm shy at speaking before an audience just as Odysseus is shy at fighting. But you all know that I'm better on the battlefield. I'm the descendant of Zeus, cousin to Achilles and of the blood of the gods. Odysseus, if you all remember, acted insane to escape fighting. He left Nestor for dead. It was I who rescued old Nestor. It was I who threw a huge boulder at Hector while Odysseus stood watching! He stole Athena's statue while all of us were fighting to the death! Now that is not a man to wear the mighty armour of Achilles. He is all tricks and cunning - too soft for the spear and sword of Achilles. Look at his shield, O Greeks! It's brand new and shining. But mine is dented and scratched from the innumerable wars that I've fought. Remember friends, words are of no use to us right now. We need swords!" There was a loud cheering for Ajax and his bravery.

Odysseus slowly rose to his feet. He glanced at the ground, then at the captains and offered a gesture of respect. Then he began, "O noble Greeks, if your prayers and mine had been heard, there'd be no debate today. Achilles would be here with us in his armour and I would be cheering him!" Odysseus dried his tears and continued, "Who's better fit to wear Achilles' armour than the one who called him out to fight? Are Greeks stupid enough to not cheer a man for intellect? My brains are always at your service. I am the son of Laertes and grandson of Arcesius who is the son of Zeus. My mother is a descendant of Hermes. I have the blood of the gods from both my parents. If you're going to give the armour to Achilles' bloodline, give it to Pyrrhus or Teucer who are related to Peleus. I was the one who talked Agamemnon into sacrificing his daughter so we could have a safe journey! I persuaded Achilles to join the war! I designed the trenches running around the Greek camps. I acted as a spy and ambassador. I did not see Ajax risking his life like me. Did Ajax stop the Greek forces from turning their ships home? Did Ajax kill the forces of King Rhesus? I remember it was brave Diomed and me! Ajax says his shield is dented, let me show you my chest..." Odysseus took off his tunic and showed his bare chest full of scars.

The crowd murmured appreciation at the scars. Then Odysseus said, "Nobody could fight Hector alone. We all drew lots that day and it fell to Ajax. Achilles was your wall, remember this. It was I who carried his body to safety. Look! Look at the shield of Achilles! Can Ajax understand the legends carved upon it? Can he read the inscriptions? It's true that I acted insane because Penelope's love held me home. You all know I have left my infant son like many of you. I took the statue of Athena from the Trojan temple so that the Trojans would not be supported by the goddess. Could Ajax glide past the priests and guards in darkness? You needed my tricks then! Ajax, your strength is that of the flesh, mine is that of the mind. And remember that the mind has greater powers over the matter. O noble Greeks, if you do not deem me worthy, then give the armour of Achilles to her!" here Odysseus pointed to the marble statue of Athena.

Of course, Odysseus was a better orator than Ajax. Look at the way he speaks - he begins with a salutation, he sheds tears, shows his scars, praises Achilles, praises many notable warriors, states his achievements and moves the hearts of the spectators. Ajax mentioned mere facts but Odysseus touched upon feelings. He received Achilles' armour. Ajax could not take it. He cried, "No one but Ajax can defeat Ajax" and plunged his sword into his heart. The noble hero died because he could not face failure in the words of Odysseus.

CHAPTER FORTY-TWO

THE TROJAN HORSE

"'Ground down by the war and driven back by Fate,
the Greek captains had watched the years slip by
until, helped by Minerva's superhuman skill,
they built that mammoth horse, immense as a
mountain,
lining its ribs with ship timbers hewn from pine.
An offering to secure safe passage home, or so
they pretend, and the story spreads through Troy.
But they pick by lot the best, most able-bodied men
and stealthily lock them into the horse's dark flanks
till the vast hold of the monster's womb is packed
with soldiers bristling weapons.'" Virgil, *Aeneid* [74-75]

The idea of the Trojan Horse was that of Odysseus, king of Ithaca. As Homer and Ovid mention nothing of this ingenious device, the tale now shifts to that of Virgil. The *Aeneid* fills the gaps left by *Iliad* and *Odyssey*. Aeneas, one of the noble warriors of Troy, fled the war and escaped carrying his sick father on his shoulder and his household gods under his arm. His ship made port at the northern shores of Africa in a little city called Carthage. This ancient city was ruled by Queen Dido who was hospitable to the fleeing Trojans. She hosted a feast during which Aeneas narrated the fall of Troy. Aeneas told the tale, seated on the guest's place of honour among the nobles of Carthage. It was unspeakable sorrow for him to flee from the agony of his countrymen and leave them to their fates.

After the death of Hector, the Greeks failed to pass over the imposing Trojan Wall (remember that it was built by Apollo and Poseidon). Odysseus came up with an idea inspired by the goddess Athena. When the Trojans found the horse, there was no one except one Greek soldier lying nearby, his arms tied behind his back. His name was Sinon and he was chosen as a sacrifice. Since the Greeks had come to Troy safely after sacrificing Iphigeneia, they decided to offer Sinon as a blood sacrifice to return home safely. Only this time, Odysseus had suggested abandoning Sinon to the Trojans who would surely kill him.

Sinon said that the Greeks had left the horse as an offering to Athena for their safe passage home. Thymoetes, a Trojan, said that the horse must be dragged inside and left on the hills as it was sacred to Athena. Cassandra (daughter of Priam blessed with foresight) warned them that it was evil and advised them to burn it. Laocoön, a Trojan priest, ran toward the men dragging it and said, "You are doomed, you fools! Do you think the enemy has sailed away? Or that Greeks, even gift-bearing ones, are free of trickery? Believe me, either the Greeks are hiding inside the horse or the horse must be a battering ram of sorts. Never trust the Greeks, especially gift-bearing ones." But of course, no one listened. Sinon was pitied and even taken inside the wall with the horse. Priam cried, "Haul Athena's effigy into our city! We shall celebrate a victory today!"

Four times the horse lurched to a halt. But the oblivious Trojans pulled with all their might and left it on the city hill, near Priam's palace. The Trojans slept peacefully that night. They did not know that the cunning Greeks had hidden their ships in the harbour of Tenedos. They did not know that the belly of the horse carried the best of the Greek soldiers. The false Sinon signalled the Greek ships after opening the city gates. Sinon opened the secret latch in the horse's belly and out came the soldiers led by Odysseus. Out came Thessandrus, Sthenelaus, Acamas, Neoptolemus (son of Achilles), Machaon, Menelaus and Epeus, the man who had made the horse. They butchered the guards and rejoined with their army entering through the gates.

The Greeks set Troy on fire. They slaughtered the sleeping Trojans and plundered what they could. Hector's ghost appeared to Aeneas and said, "Escape, son of Aphrodite, tear yourself from the flames! Take your household gods and your comrades. Seek a city for the Trojans and once you have roved the seas, erect strong walls in our new home!" Aeneas saw sights horrible while he escaped - a group of Greeks dragging Cassandra by the hair, the temple of Apollo desecrated and the palace of Priam ruined. Old Priam wore his armour and girded his sword. Hecuba and her daughters were hiding around Apollo's altar. Polites (the last surviving son of Priam) was with them. Cruel Neoptolemus slit Polites' throat before the eyes of Priam and Hecuba. Neoptolemus lifted Priam onto the altar and stabbed him. Thus ended the life of a noble king, a great leader and a wise ruler. Hecuba was taken to be distributed as spoils of war.

The wealthy court of Polymestor was located in Bistones, a city not far from Troy. Priam had sent his son Polydorus and his daughter Polyxena there. He trusted Polymestor to keep them safe from the Greeks. Priam had sent Polymestor chests of gold regularly as payment. When the gold dwindled, wicked Polymestor caught Polydorus and slit his throat. He then tossed the body into the sea. The ghost of Achilles appeared to Agamemnon and said, "You have forgotten me after death. Bring Polyxena here! Her sacrifice will decorate my tomb." The Greeks took his words and brought the girl from Bistones. Hecuba curled around her daughter, the last surviving descendant of Ilus, the founder of Troy. Neoptolemus ripped her from her mother's arms but the maiden did not cry. She told Neoptolemus that she would walk.

Polyxena walked to the tomb of Achilles and faced Neoptolemus. Then she said, "Your sword has choice of either throat or chest. I shall not be the servant of men. Let not my mother know the way I died. Her sorrow makes my death less glorious. If I have the right to ask this favour, then let no man touch my body. I am the daughter of Priam, the descendant of Ilus. Let my body be removed by my mother's maids. Ask not money from my mother for she has already paid much in tears." Polyxena stood tall and steady as Neoptolemus lifted his sword. All those who saw her wept for her. But her eyes were dry; her feet did not tremble. Neoptolemus drove his sword into her brave heart. Even as she fell, her white face maintained decorum and her falling arms drew her dress over to cover her body.

The Greeks had never seen such a brave girl who walked to her death. The Greeks allowed the Trojan women to carry her body to Hecuba. The mother poured her tears over her daughter's wound and her white hair was stained red with her daughter's blood. She said bitterly, "O my dear child, the last of all, they murdered even you. The damned Achilles' ghost pursues us even after death! All the children of my womb are dead by his hand! Troy lies burned! My tears are your wreath and your tomb the sanded waste of some foreign shore." Then a sudden rage took over her. Possessed with a fury, she began snarling and biting like an animal. She ran to Polymestor's palace and scratched out his eyes. The guards threw their spears and stones at her. She barked at them and the gods transformed her into a dog.

CHAPTER FORTY-THREE

GLAUCUS AND CIRCE

"Circe went white with rage (an understatement)
Yet could not strike at Glaucus (for she loved him)
And turned her violent mind against the girl:" Ovid,
Metamorphoses Book XIV [376]

There was a skilled fisherman in the city of Anthedon and his name was Glaucus. One day, he toiled very hard and decided to wander into the woods. These woods were near a bay and he saw strange herbs growing. The cattle of Helios were grazing nearby and none of them took a bite of these herbs. Glaucus sat down among these herbs and lay down to rest. His catch lay near his feet, all silvery and glittery. Suddenly, they began jumping again, being brought back to life by the touch of these miraculous herbs. Glaucus plucked a leaf and popped it in his mouth. He ate the bitter herb and got what he wanted. He became immortal but his legs vanished. A huge slimy fish tail grew in their place. His hands sprouted fins and he became a merman. He swam out to the sea. What a surprise! He could breathe underwater. And the ocean deities welcomed him to their underwater palace. Oceanus and Tethys washed him in a hundred sheets of water and chanted hymns nine times around him. They taught him the art of prophecy and Glaucus became a god.

The problem came soon and in the form of a woman. On a beautiful evening when the sunlight was just right, Scylla came out to listen to the stories of her friends. Scylla was a beautiful nymph who often wandered naked on the seashore. That evening, she heard a loud conch blowing and saw Glaucus looking at her from behind a moss-covered rock. He was madly in love with her and confessed his feelings for her. He said, "Dear girl, sweet nymph, I'm neither man nor fish. I have been made a god, far superior to Proteus or Triton. . ." but Scylla ran away before he could complete. Then Glaucus had an idea. He decided to go to Circe, the famed witch, and ask her help.

Circe was the daughter of Helios and Perse. She was an Oceanid and a sister of Aeëtes, Medea's father (remember Jason and the Golden Fleece?). But more than that, she was a powerful sorceress with a special talent for metamorphosing men into animals. Circe had several lovers who later faced her fury. These poor men were transformed into beasts and locked up beneath her cottage. In Homer's *Odyssey*, she changes Odysseus' crew into pigs and the hero has to get the help of the god Hermes to change them back. Going to Circe was not a good idea because she was cunning and unpredictable. Poor Glaucus swam into her green-hilled island and saw her mixing herbs. He said to her, "Dear goddess, you alone can help me. I'm in love with Scylla and you're good with herbs. Please give her some herbs that will make her love me."

Poor Glaucus did not know that Circe had an eye on him. She glared at him and said, "Go find a girl or woman who's inclined to be eager like you. Even better, you can take me, a full-grown goddess who can please you with charms." Glaucus was shocked and replied, "Lady, trees shall grow in the sea and seaweed on the mountains before my love for Scylla fades away." Wrong decision. Poor choice of words. Glaucus swam away in shame and anger. But Circe held her grudges. She decided to take vengeance on poor Scylla. Circe blended some herbs and sang incantations to Hecate. She dressed in blue and ran through her home where pigs, dogs and lions leaped up to kiss her feet. She came to where Scylla lived and saw the girl. Scylla favoured a little pool of water hidden among the rocks. She used to bathe here. Circe understood this and came to the pool before the nymph. She poured her magic potion into the pool. She said her spell nine times and danced thrice. Then she vanished.

When Scylla came to the pool, she splashed waist-deep in the coolness. Then to her horror, her legs were gone. She saw a girdle of barking dogs' heads around her womb. There were dogs around her breasts also. Glaucus saw her and wept. He realised his mistake in involving Circe. Scylla became a monster and devoured sailors who passed by her rock. In Homer's *Odyssey*, Scylla eats many of the hero's crew. She lives near Charybdis, a maelstrom that tears ships to pieces. Both Scylla and Charybdis were considered horrors by sailors who passed by.

Note: 'Between Scylla and Charybdis' is an idiom derived from these monsters. It is used to refer to a situation where you are trapped between two evils/ challenges. 'Stuck between the devil and the deep blue sea' is a similar proverb.

CHAPTER FORTY-FOUR

THE MAN OF VERSATILE WITS

"'Cyclops, if any one asks you who it was that put your eye out and spoiled your beauty, say it was the valiant warrior Odysseus, son of Laertes, who lives in Ithaca.'" Homer, *Odyssey* Book IX [561]

The legendary walled city of Troy lay in ruins, fire leaping up from her highest towers and ashes dancing across the twilight sky. The Greeks revelled in their victory over the Trojans and sang their battle songs. They sacrificed Trojan victims to demigods and cult heroes and offered hecatombs[48] to the gods. Agamemnon, the commander of the Greek forces, stood on the prow of his ship, his face gleaming in pride. The lower decks of his ship were bursting with spoils - Trojan gold, ornaments from temples, rare goblets inlaid with silver and mother-of-pearl, cauldrons, tripods, swords as shiny as the moon on a starless sky, bronze-tipped spears and incomparably beautiful women. Menelaus had got what he wanted; Helen was aboard his ship and he had got many other treasures also. They were ready to return home after ten years of battle. But the gods were not happy.

Athena, goddess of heroes, chariots, war and wisdom was specifically furious with two men - Odysseus and Diomedes. Why? Because they had stolen the Palladium from Troy. Now this Palladium was a sacred image of Athena that protected Troy from invaders. The Greeks were able to win only after Odysseus and Diomedes got hold of it. Odysseus, who was often called the "Versatile Man" or the "Man of Many Wits" came up with the Trojan Horse idea after stealing the Palladium. Now that they had won, the Greeks were afraid of sailing back. What if the goddess created storms and shipwrecked them all? The sons of Atreus (Agamemnon and Menelaus) called a meeting to discuss the matter. Menelaus wanted to sail home immediately. Agamemnon wanted to offer hecatombs to Athena to please her. The Greeks were heavy with wine and the meeting was adjourned. The next day, half of them sailed away with Menelaus before sunrise. Odysseus was one of them.

The island of Tenedos was chosen by Menelaus to offer prayers on the way back to Greece. However, there was a big quarrel and Odysseus went back to join Agamemnon's ships that still lay in the Trojan harbour. The hero sailed home with Agamennon's contingent but Athena and Zeus separated his ships. Fate had set many ill adventures in store for Odysseus. The wind took him to Ismarus, the city of the Cicons, a race of warriors. The Greeks took much booty and women but the Cicons called for reinforcements and Odysseus lost many men in battle. They sailed away but Zeus raised the North Wind against them. The wind tore their sails off and they were forced to drop anchor off Cape Malea by the island of Cythera. After ten days, they reached the island of the Lotos-Eaters. These people ate food prepared with a bulb called 'Lotos'. Please note that they did not eat the lotus flower. They offered their food to some of Odysseus' sailors and they all forgot their duty to return home. Odysseus grabbed them and forced them aboard their ships. They wept and wailed as the ships left the shore. The third adventure proved fatal for many of Odysseus' men.

The island of the Cyclopes was uninhabited, dark and forlorn. There were no farms or plantations. The crops there were wild wheat, barley and grapes growing to a height reachable by no human hand. There were wild goats that roamed the island in peace. Since the island had a good harbour and clean water springs, Odysseus ordered his men to drop anchor and fill up their supplies. They hunted the wild goats and carried them aboard. Odysseus had twelve ships and each ship had nine goats. Odysseus took ten goats. They got out their spits and cauldrons and cooked the goats on the beach. They drank the wine they took from the Cicons. At daybreak, Odysseus called a meeting and said, "Stay here, my brave warriors! This island looks fertile but we do not know what manner of men or beasts inhabit it. I will take a small group and explore the island. The rest of you remain in your ships."

Odysseus and his exploratory team went up the hills and saw caves, lots and lots of caves carved into the rocky cliffs. They went near a cave and saw that it was overhung with laurels. There was a large yard with many wild sheep and goats. The cave was well-shaded with pine and oak trees. They went inside and saw that the cave was lined neatly with racks of cheese. There were hundreds of pails brimming with thick milk. The team wanted to steal everything and get back to the ships. But Odysseus hoped to wait and meet the master of the cave so that he might receive a gift. Little did he realise that death was on the way. The team ate cheese and went to sleep. Soon they heard a thudding sound. The master was a Cyclopes, a giant with just one eye on his forehead. He entered the cave and drove all the animals to their pens. Then he blocked the cave with a huge boulder. He saw the men inside his cave and said, "Strangers, who are you? Where do you hail from? Are you merchants, explorers or conquerors?"

"We are Acheans on our way from Troy. We are the people of Agamemnon, who is famous for sacking Troy and burning it to the ground. We are a race of noble warriors bound homeward to Greece. We humbly pray to you for hospitality as we are your supplicants under the wreath of Zeus," replied Odysseus. Supplicants were believed to be under the protection of Zeus himself and no one would dare hurt them. Odysseus thought this might offer him some protection.

"Stranger, we care naught for your gods for we are of a race stronger than they are. You are fools for you do not know that we have neither laws nor rituals to appease the gods," said the Cyclopes. As he spoke, he bent down, grabbed two men and dashed them to the ground. Their brains were shed upon the ground and their blood drenched the floor of the cave. The giant tore them limb from limb and ate them, munching slowly upon their bones and entrails. Then he drank all the pails of milk and slept soundly. Odysseus and the others were horrified. They couldn't do anything to save their friends. Odysseus thought of stabbing the giant with his sword but only the giant could lift the boulder blocking the cave. So Odysseus sat down and thought. He thought long and deep till he came up with a plan.

At dawn, the Cyclopes grabbed two more men and ate them for breakfast. He then left after blocking the entrance to the cave. Odysseus saw a huge olive tree trunk lying inside the cave. He cut six feet length off of it and told the men to sharpen one end of it. He charred the sharp point over a fire to harden it and hid it away. At dusk, the Cyclopes entered the cave and blocked his exit again. He snatched two more men and ate them for supper. Odysseus offered the giant some wine and he accepted it. "This is exquisite! Give me the whole cask of wine, stranger! And tell me your name so that I can give you a gift," said the giant. Odysseus offered him the whole barrel that he had brought with his provisions and said, "My name is Outis ('nobody' in Greek)." Drunk with black wine, the giant roared, "Outis, I will eat you last after all your friends. This is my gift to you. Ha, ha, ha!"

That night, the Cyclopes lay snoring in his cave. Odysseus chose four of his best men and brought the hardened stake they had made from the olive wood. They heated the sharp point over the embers and plunged it deep into the giant's eye. They bore down their weight and kept turning it round and round as it dug into the monster's eye. The Cyclopes roared in pain and anger. His blood spilled over the wood and the steam from the eyeball scalded his eyelid and eyebrow. The eyeball hissed and sputtered over the wood. The other Cyclopes who lived in the nearby caves woke up and called to him, "What ails you, Polyphemus? Why are you roaring in the middle of the night? Who is troubling or robbing you by force?"

Polyphemus, for that was the Cyclopes' name, replied "Outis (Nobody) is troubling me or robbing me by force!" Since 'nobody' was hurting him, they went back to their caves and slept soundly. No one came to his rescue.

Polyphemus pulled out the stake from his burning eye and threw the boulder away from the entrance. He then sat down at the entrance and opened his arms wide to catch Odysseus and the others as they slipped out. Odysseus had thought of this also. He told his men to climb onto the backs of the wild sheep inside the cave. Polyphemus did not mind his sheep and drove them outside the cave. When Odysseus and his men got aboard their ships safely, Odysseus called out to the Cyclopes. "Cyclopes, if anyone asks you who it was that put your eye out, tell them it was Odysseus, son of Laertes and King of Ithaca." Polyphemus hurled rocks at the ships but Odysseus steered away. Then the Cyclopes prayed to Poseidon who was none other than his father. Poseidon heard the prayer and remembered to let Odysseus have a tough time sailing home.

CHAPTER FORTY-FIVE

THE DAUGHTER OF THE SUN

> "'Your men are shut up in Circe's pig-styes, like so many wild boars in their lairs. You surely do not fancy that you can set them free. I can tell you that you will never get back and will have to stay there with the rest of them.'"
> Homer, *Odyssey* Book X [570]

Odysseus sailed for many days and prayed to many gods for safe passage but Poseidon's wrath brought him woe. The Versatile Man reached the Aeolian island ruled by Aeolus. According to the custom of the island, Aeolus' six sons married his six daughters and lived in their grand castle. They had feasts every day and the castle did not lack any manner of luxury. Odysseus stayed with Aeolus for a whole month and at the end, the king offered Odysseus a gift. Aeolus had power over the winds. So he caught the four winds and shut them up in a special bag made of ox-hide and offered it to Odysseus so he could sail home faster. Odysseus sailed for ten days and saw the horizon of Ithaca looming in the distance. Odysseus' crew became jealous and thought that Aeolus had given their captain gold and jewels. They opened the ox-hide bag while Odysseus was asleep and all the winds came howling forth and raised a storm. The ships were tossed about and Odysseus found himself back on Aeolus' island. But the king refused to help him a second time. "You are a disgrace to mankind! Surely the gods have cursed you and I cannot undo your sins!" said Aeolus.

Six nights did they sail before reaching the island of Telephylus, home of the Laestrygonians or the sheep-herders. Odysseus sent his scouts to find out who ruled the land. They were shocked to see a giantess who was queen of the island. As soon as she laid eyes on Odysseus' scouts, she called out to her husband Antiphates who set about killing them. The Laestrygonians were nasty ogres who came running out to slaughter Odysseus' crew. They speared them like fishes and roasted them on spits. Odysseus cut the cable of his ship and sailed away as fast as he could. After many days, they reached the island of Aeaea. There was a safe harbour for the ships and the island was beautiful. It was ruled by Circe, a legendary sorceress who was the daughter of the Titan Helios and the nymph Perse. She was the sister of Aeëtes (keeper of the Golden Fleece and Medea's father) and Pasiphaë (wife of Minos). And she had already seen Odysseus arrive.

Odysseus divided his men into two groups and made Eurylochus the captain of one while he led the other. They cast lots in a helmet and it was Eurylochus' turn to explore the island. Odysseus kept the ships ready in case they needed to escape. Eurylochus and his team went deep into the wooded island. They saw smoke rising in the distance and went closer. They spotted a beautiful cottage built with cut stones and all manner of wild animals - lions, wolves and bears - prowling about the house. But these animals did not attack the men, rather they wagged their tails and rubbed their noses lovingly against them. These beasts were in fact mortal men who had been bewitched by the cunning Circe. On nearing the gates, they heard a woman singing melodiously inside. They peeped into the cottage and saw a strikingly beautiful woman on the loom weaving a tapestry with a hundred splendid colours that only a goddess could do. They knocked on the door and Circe opened it. She made them welcome and offered them fresh cheese, honey, bread and Pramnian wine. The men were extremely hungry and ate ravenously. Eurylochus suspected foul play and did not touch the food. Circe had actually drugged the wine and as they drank, they forgot their homes and stayed with her. She waved her wand and lo! they were all transformed into pigs. She shut them up in her pig styes and threw them acorns to eat. Eurylochus ran back to Odysseus and told him everything. The hero girded his bronze sword and took his bow. He leaped onto the shore and went forth to save his friends, leaving Eurylochus in charge of the ships.

While Odysseus was marching forward to rescue his friends, he spotted a handsome young man in the forest. It was the god Hermes with his golden wand. The god said, "Whither are you going, Odysseus? Your men are now the slaves of Circe. You cannot save them as she is very powerful."

"Hail Hermes, saviour and messenger of the Olympians! I may not be able to save them but I must try. After all, they are my friends and have bound their allegiances to me," said Odysseus.

"Then take this herb. It is called "moly" and it will protect you from her sorcery. Mortals cannot uproot this herb. When you meet her, she will mix a drink for you. Of course, the drink is enchanted with her magic but the herb will protect you. Then she will use her wand and at that moment, you must spring upon her with your sword in your hand. She will be frightened and desire you to sleep with her. You must not refuse her but make her swear a solemn oath by all the gods so that she may not practise any magic on you," said Hermes and drew out the milky white herb from his robe. Odysseus took the herb and went into Circe's cottage.

Circe welcomed Odysseus warmly and sat him on a silver-inlaid seat with a matching footstool. She offered him wine in a golden golden goblet and he drank it. Then she took out her wand and waved it over him. But he rushed at her and held her down with his sword. Circe was terribly frightened at this and fell to his knees. "Who or what are you, stranger? How are you able to resist my charms? Surely no man has withstood my magic before! You must be none other than the bold Odysseus. Hermes always said you would stop by my island one day and it is true. So be it; sheathe your sword and come with me so that we may be friends."

"But how can I trust you? You must swear an oath on all the gods not to harm me," said Odysseus. Circe swore the oath and they slept together. The sorceress and her maids took good care of Odysseus after that. A group of nymphs laid the table and bread was brought forth in golden baskets. They mixed wine in silver goblets. Circe gave a good cloak and a shirt to Odysseus. After the meal, she took him to her pig-styes and rubbed an unguent on the pigs. They were transformed back to their original selves. Odysseus and the others stayed with Circe for a whole year feasting and celebrating. After a year, Odysseus was reminded of his homeward journey and asked Circe for directions.

"Odysseus, noble son of Laertes, you cannot return home without first consulting the blind prophet Tiresias. You must go to the Underworld and consult the ghost of Tiresias. He is the only ghost who still retains his knowledge. Persephone has gifted him even in death. He is the one who can guide you home," said Circe. Odysseus was horrified and wept bitterly as no mortal could enter the Underworld. The journey itself was perilous as was the return. Circe guided him further, "Raise your mast and the North Wind will fill your white sails. You will reach the white waters of the Underworld after sailing across the river Oceanus. You will find two rivers Phlegethon and Cocytus flowing into the fiery Acheron. You will see a rock near it. Here you must dig a trench and pour a drink offering to the dead. Pour honey mixed with milk first, then wine and last water. Sprinkle white barley meal over the whole. When you see the ghosts come to drink, pray to them and promise to sacrifice a barren heifer to them when you return to Ithaca. Promise Tiresias that you will sacrifice a black sheep. Offer a ram and a black ewe to Hades and Persephone on the spot. Let the blood run into the trench. Tiresias will come to you and guide you."

Odysseus and his men feasted well and rested till dawn. At sunrise, Circe dressed in a gossamer robe and girdled her waist with a golden belt. She then brought them all manners of food and provisions for their journey ahead. She also brought a ram and black ewe to be sacrificed to Hades. However, they had totally forgotten about Elpenor, a sailor who had drunk too heavily the previous night. Elpenor had fallen from Circe's roof and died. But the others were too busy going home and left poor Elpenor without a decent funeral. Elpenor's ghost was already down in the Underworld waiting for Odysseus to come.

CHAPTER FORTY-SIX

THE JOURNEY TO THE UNDERWORLD

"'. . . whereon the ghosts came trooping up from Erebus - brides, young bachelors, old men worn out with toil, maids who had been crossed in love, and brave men who had been killed in battle, with their armour still smirched with blood; they came from every quarter and flitted around the trench with a strange kind of screaming sound that made me turn pale with fear.'" Homer, *Odyssey* Book XI [579]

The sky was clear and the waves lapped gently on the shore of Aeaea. It was a perfect day to sail and Odysseus knew the winds like the back of his hands. The Greeks, guided by the sorceress Circe, sailed with full sails till they reached the dark islands of the Cimmerians. These were melancholy folk who lived in a land that was always dark. They never saw the sun nor did they know of its warmth and splendour. The Greeks left their ships and walked along the banks of the river Oceanus. They were exhausted and depressed from the voyage. They did not know if they would ever see their homes again. Nevertheless, Odysseus inspired his men to walk further to the spot where the dreaded rock stood. This was the entrance to the Underworld. Perimedes and Eurylochus led the sacrificial ram and ewe while Odysseus drug the trench. They braced themselves to face the horrid ghosts.

Odysseus poured honey and milk, wine and water, and sprinkled barley meal over the whole as instructed by Circe. Then he slit the throats of the ram and the ewe and let the blood trickle down into the trench. He stood still as he watched the red blood twirl around in the milk and flow down into the red wine. As soon as the blood ran down, the ghosts caught the scent of it and floated towards the Greeks. All sorts of ghosts flew towards them - young brides dead on their wedding day, healthy youths killed in battle, virgins who did not know the caresses of love and old folks who had died in their beds surrounded by their families. Some of them had blood oozing out of their bodies and looked horrid indeed. They flitted around the trench with a strange eerie wail that sent ice down the spines of the Greeks. But they were brave and stood their ground.

Praying to Hades and Persephone, Odysseus held his sword over the trench and did not allow the ghosts to drink the blood before he caught sight of Tiresias. The first ghost that talked to Odysseus was that of Elpenor, his poor comrade who had died falling from the roof of Circe's cottage. "Sweet Odysseus, my best comrade, I beg of you, do not leave me unburied. Offer me a proper funeral. Build a barrow on the sea shore with my armour and stick the oar that I used to row over it," wailed Elpenor. Odysseus promised him a decent burial. Then Odysseus saw the ghost of his mother Anticlea. She had been alive when he went to Troy. Even in all his sorrow, he did not let her drink the blood till he saw Tiresias. The blind prophet came presently. He was the only ghost who still looked like a human and carried his golden sceptre in his hand. He also had his knowledge and recognised Odysseus. "Noble son of Laertes, what brings you to this dismal place? Surely you are not dead! Sheathe your sword so that I may drink of the blood and answer your questions," said Tiresias. Odysseus sheathed his sword and drew back. The prophet drank his fill and uttered his prophecies through bloody lips.

"You seek safe passage back to Ithaca. But you will not escape the bitter eye of Poseidon who still holds a grudge against you for injuring his son. Still, you may reach home if you do not harm the cattle of Helios when you reach the Thrinacian island. When you get home you will get your revenge on all the suitors who demand your wife's hand. Later when you reclaim your land, you must take a well-made oar and walk till you reach a country whose people have never seen the sea. A passer-by will meet you and mistake your oar for a shovel. You must fix the oar on the ground where you meet the passer-by and sacrifice a ram, a bull and a heifer to Poseidon. Then go back to Ithaca and offer sacrifices to all the gods. As for your own death, it will come from the sea. You will die old and full of years and peace of mind. It will be a gentle death and you will rest in peace," said Tiresias.

Once Tiresias left the trench, Odysseus allowed the ghosts to drink the blood. Anticlea recognised her son as soon as she tasted the blood. "My son, what dark fate has brought you here to this gloom? Are you returning from Troy? Have you been home and seen your wife?" she asked.

"Mother dear, I am here because I had to consult the prophet Tiresias. Now I have a way home. But tell me, and tell me true, how is Penelope? Tell me also about my poor father and my sweet son. And tell me the manner of your death," asked Odysseus.

"Your faithful wife is tormented by the suitors who ruin your estate. She has not yet consented to marry any of them. Your son Telemachus still holds your estate. Your father lives in his country home and never goes near town. As for me, I was not gifted with a swift death. Nor did I die of disease or old age. I died because I longed for you," said Anticlea and Odysseus tried to embrace her. But she flitted through him like smoke. After Anticlea left the rock, Odysseus saw a host of women - they were once popular women when they were alive.

The beautiful Tyro came first. She was raped by Poseidon and bore Pelias and Neleus, both of who served Zeus. Next came Antiope, the lover of Zeus and whose sons Amphion and Zethus founded the seven-gated Thebes. Then came Alcmena, the mother of Hercules and Megara, the first wife of Hercules. Jocasta, the mother and wife of Oedipus came lingering behind. Leda, the mother of Helen was next. Ariadne, the fair daughter of Minos came next. All of them drank the blood and flew away, some of them wailing dreadfully and some silently.

The ghost of Agamemnon appeared sad and stretched out its arms to embrace Odysseus after drinking the blood. Odysseus wept for his commander and said, "King Agamemnon? How came you by your death? Did Poseidon raise his waters and wreck your ships? Or did you die in some other battle?"

"Odysseus, noble son of Laertes, I was not lost at sea nor did I die honourably in battle. But my wife Clytemnestra and her wicked lover Aegisthus[49] slaughtered me in my very chamber! She drugged my wine and he slaughtered me and my comrades like swine. My wife did not even close my eyes as I was dying. Be not too friendly with your own wife and keep your own counsel. But tell me, and tell me true, is there any news of my son Orestes[50]?" said Agamemnon with a groan. Unfortunately, Odysseus did not know anything about Orestes as he was lost at sea. But Orestes had indeed avenged his father and killed Aegisthus.

Then came Achilles, with the ghosts of Patroclus, Antilochus and Ajax - all of them strong and powerful even in death. "Odysseus, noble son of Laertes, what manner of tricks are you up to that you venture down into Hades?" asked Achilles. Odysseus told him the whole story and said that Achilles was lucky indeed as he was adored by all the Greeks. "Say nothing of that sort. It is better to be a slave in a nobleman's house than king of the dead. But what news about my son Neoptolemus[51]?" said the hero of the Trojan War.

"I took Neoptolemus in my own ship and sailed from Scyros. He is a wise boy and full of valour. He always spoke first in meetings and dashed to fight in the front line at war. He killed many valiant heroes and got plenty of booty. He returned home safe without a scratch on him," said Odysseus. The ghost of Achilles was very pleased and flew away in pride.

The ghost of Ajax stood away from Odysseus because of the argument over Achilles' armour. Odysseus tried to pacify him but he turned away. Then Odysseus saw Minos with his golden sceptre. Hades had made Minos one of the judges of the dead because of his wisdom. All the ghosts were gathered around him, waiting for their judgements. Then he saw Orion[52], the hunter chasing all the ghosts of the beasts he had killed. There was Tantalus[53] who stood in a lake full of water. But if he tried to drink it, the water level came down and the whole lake dried up. There was Sisyphus[54] who rolled the enormous boulder time and again over a mountain once it rolled down. Last of all, he saw the shade of Hercules who had come down from Olympus with his beautiful wife Hebe. He saw Theseus also. But after all this Odysseus was frightened that evil spirits, furies or gorgons might come out. So he hastened with his men towards the ships and lifted the anchor quickly.

CHAPTER FORTY-SEVEN

LAND OF THE SIRENS, SCYLLA AND CHARYBDIS

"'If any one unwarily draws in too close and hears the singing of the Sirens, his wife and children will never welcome him home again, for they sit in a green field and warble him to death with the sweetness of their song. There is a great heap of dead men's bones lying all around, with the flesh still rotting off them.'" Homer, *Odyssey* Book XII [595]

The Underworld shrunk behind as Odysseus and his crew sailed away into the light. They breathed a sigh of relief as the Aeaean island came gliding slowly upon the horizon. It was morning and the rosy-fingered Aurora rose steadily upon the east, shedding her kindly rays upon all who lived and breathed. Odysseus went straight to Circe's house and got Elpenor's body. The crew lamented and performed his funeral rites. When his body and armour had been burnt to ashes, they raised a cairn and set a stone over it. Then they fixed his oar upon the stone.

Circe dressed herself in a splendid gossamer silk gown and threw a gold-embroidered robe around her high shoulders. She tied her robes with a gold girdle and ordered her maids to serve the sailors bread, meat and wine. They feasted to their heart's content and at dusk, she led Odysseus to her private chamber. There she listened to his adventures and said, "Odysseus, it is good that you have endured so much with bravery. But the worst is yet to come. Listen to me and listen well. To get home, you must take the path that leads straight to the island of the Sirens. These are beautiful women who have wings. They will lure you with their melodious songs, then snatch you off the ships and eat you. Pass them by and stop your men's ears with wax. If you want to listen to their songs, get your men to bind you to the mast. They must never listen when you beg and pray to them to release you. On no occasion must you untie yourself.

"Once you have sailed past the Sirens, you will reach a couple of huge rocks called the Wanderers. These rocks crush anything that passes through them. Not even a bird can fly through them. The only ship that sailed through them was the Argo and that was because Hera guided Jason safely. One of the rocks goes high into the heavens and it is impossible to climb. There is a cavern in between and you must take your ships this way. The cavern faces West towards the Underworld. Inside it sits Scylla[55]; a horrible monster. She has twelve feet and six necks that are long and flexible like serpents. At the end of each neck, she has a frightful head with three rows of teeth. No ship can sail past without losing some people to her. She leaps to the edge and carries off a man in each mouth.

"The rock is lower but so close together that not even an arrow can fly through them. A large fig tree grows upon it and below this tree lies the sucking whirlpool called Charybdis. The vortex twists so fast and lashes out the water three times a day. The same vortex spins in the opposite direction and then sucks the water back in so deep that not even Poseidon himself can escape from the depths. You must steer towards Scylla's side and away from Charybdis. It is better to lose six men than an entire crew. It will be hard but if you call out the name of Crataiis, Scylla's mom, then the monster may stop reaching for your men a second time.

If you survive all these, you will reach the Thrinacian island. You will see herds of cattle and flocks of sheep that belong to Helios. These cattle do not breed nor do they die. They are tended by the daughters of Helios. You must leave these cattle unharmed and you will reach Ithaca. Harm them and you will face a terrible fate," Circe ended her instructions and the crew got ready. They set sail at dawn and Circe cast a fair wind to help them sail safe and steady.

Odysseus told his crew everything that Circe had told him. By the time he was finished, they neared the rocks inhabited by the Sirens. All of a sudden, the wind dropped and the sea turned dead calm. Odysseus took a large reel of wax and cut it into pieces with his dagger. He offered it to the men and they stuffed their ears. Then they tied their captain to the mast. The Sirens were all female, lovely as angels and flew around with beautiful wings. They sang songs about Odysseus' triumphant return from Troy. Odysseus wept and screamed to be released but Eurylochus tied him tighter. When they had crossed over safely, they took off the wax and released Odysseus who thanked them for not untying him.

Suddenly, there was a huge roar and a crash! It sounded as though the Earth had cracked and the waters flowed inward into the crack. They left off rowing and Odysseus saw the Wanderers and how they crashed. Odysseus steered towards the cavern of Scylla and saw below. Charybdis sucked in water with such force and when the water was released, it boiled and turned red. The water sizzled and hissed like a thousand slimy snakes. The bottom of the whirlpool was full of sharp rocks, black and deadly. Odysseus put on his armour and stood ready to cut off Scylla's neck. As they were watching the whirlpool, Scylla pounced down and took off six men in her jaws. The others could do nothing but listen to their screams. This was the most soul-crushing sight Odysseus had seen in his entire voyage.

The crew got out of the Wanderers and reached the noble home of Helios. They saw the immortal cattle and Odysseus made them swear oaths to leave the animals alone. They went further inland and ate the food given by Circe. They were forced to remain there for a month as the wind blew only towards the South and the East. The food was gone and the men grew restless. Eurylochus called the crew and said to them, "Listen, comrades. This island is full of worthy meat and we are starving. Let us eat the cattle and later we will build a temple to Helios and offer him hecatombs." The others cheered him and hunted down the cows. They prayed to Helios and slaughtered the cows. They cut out the thigh bones and wrapped them in two layers of meat and offered it to Helios. They placed more meat over it and poured water over the sacrifice as they did not have any wine. They placed the inner organs and other meat over spits and roasted them finely.

Odysseus woke up with the smell of cooking meat and rushed to the spot. He cursed the men and himself for sleeping. Helios was terribly angry and went up to Zeus. He said, "Father Zeus, Odysseus and his men have slaughtered my cattle. If you do not do anything, I will go down to the Underworld and shine among the dead."

"Helios, go on shining upon us gods and among man. I will send a bolt of lightning and shiver the ships into pieces of wood," said Zeus. Odysseus scolded his crew and got them abroad quickly. The meat began mooing like cows once it was cooked. The hide crawled about like snakes. Zeus struck them with his mighty thunder and all the ships broke into tiny pieces. Most of the crew drowned. Odysseus clung to a piece of the mast and swam with all his might. He was carried back to Charybdis. He waited patiently for the whirlpool to vomit out its waters and he used this to swim out again. He drifted for nine days and reached the island of Ogygia on the tenth day. Little did he know that he would be a captive of Ogygian Calypso for seven years.

CHAPTER FORTY-EIGHT

The Nymph of the Plaited Tresses

"I stayed with Calypso seven years straight on end, and watered the good clothes she gave me with my tears the whole time, but at last when the eighth year came round she bade me depart of her own free will, either because Jove had told her she must, or because she had changed her mind." Homer, *Odyssey* Book VII [530]

The sea was rough and stormy, dark and full of ire. The waters gurgled and boiled around whirlpools and jagged rocks. Odysseus, utterly exhausted and frustrated with his misfortune, let the waves take him to his fate, whatever it may be. He lay prostrate upon a piece of timber, the mast of his beloved ship and watched the sky. Suddenly, he jerked up and tumbled upon the sand. He had landed on the beautiful shores of Ogygia and it was a grand new day. The sun was shining upon the horizon and hope reignited in

Odysseus' heart. He got up and walked towards the distant trees. He saw smoke rising in the distance and walked toward it. There was a clearing in the forest and above it was a cave. The cave was sheltered by fragrant cypress trees. Creepers covered the entrance to the cave and all manners of birds lived around, singing sweetly. There was a large grapevine twisted around the entrance and it bore huge bunches of grapes. The nearby spring was channelled into four rivulets and they ran through fertile meadows where iris and celery were cultivated most skillfully. It was indeed a spot most charming even to halt a god or goddess passing by.

Odysseus neared the cave and heard a most melodious voice singing bars of some ancient forgotten hymn. The forlorn hero called out and was surprised to see a beautiful young woman step down from inside. She wore a gossamer robe that shone like the full moon on a starless sky. Her hair was twisted around her comely head in ringlets that fell over her shoulders and reached the floor. Her arms and neck were adorned with jewels that shone like the sun. She was the nymph Calypso, daughter of the Titan Atlas and known for her beautiful hair and powerful magic. She took Odysseus inside and offered him the choicest bread, cheese and meats. She sat down on her loom and sang melodiously while he ate. Her golden shuttle flashed across her hands at lightning speed and as Odysseus watched her, he forgot his home, his wife and all his adventures. Calypso had bewitched him with her powerful magical songs.

Calypso offered Odysseus the best of everything and he stayed with her for seven years. But he went and sat down by the silent sea every evening and wept. He started remembering his home little by little and hated his life with Calypso. The nymph of the beautiful tresses pulled out her trump card - she offered to make him her immortal husband if he stayed with her. He could live the life of a god. Odysseus refused outright and went to his favourite spot by the sea and lamented. Calypso had ceased to please him. The goddess Athena saw all this and spoke to Zeus. The mighty thunderer sent down Hermes to rescue the hero from the spells of Calypso. Hermes went to the nymph and she offered him sweet ambrosia and red nectar, the food that made the gods immortal. Once he had eaten, she spoke; "Hermes of the golden wand, what brings you here to Ogygia? You are most welcome and I will do what you ask of me."

"Since you ask me, I will tell you. Zeus sent me here. He says you have here with you a man tormented by misfortune for years. He had fought bravely in Troy and lost to the waves on his return home. Now Zeus bids you to release him as it is not his destiny to stay here with you but return home to his high-vaulted home," said Hermes. Calypso was outraged at this. She said, "You gods are so ruthless and jealous. You choose to love mortal women at your heart's desire. But when we women choose to love mortal men, you come down and wreak havoc. I rescued Odysseus from drowning. And now, Zeus orders me to release him. But I will obey the will of Zeus. However, I have no ships and no crew to help him." Hermes accepted and went back to Mt. Olympus.

Calypso went straight to Odysseus by the sea and said, "My friend, do not waste away your life in your tears. I will help you leave the island as that is what the gods desire. Go and fell some tall trees and make a raft to carry you across the sea. I will provide you with clothing and food and send you a favourable wind." But the crafty hero made her swear upon Styx before he followed her advice. Calypso brought a huge double-bladed axe and Odysseus cut the sturdiest trees for his raft. Next, she gave him an adze of polished steel and the hero trimmed the trees. She gave him boring tools and Odysseus fixed the logs of wood together. She even gave him cloth for the sail. It took Odysseus four days to complete the raft.

When the raft was ready to sail, Calypso brought two skins - one of dark wine and the other of water - and placed them on the boat. She also brought a sack of grain and boxes of meat. She chanted a spell and a gentle breeze filled the sail of the raft. Odysseus set sail towards his home. He sailed for seventeen days and spotted the island of the Phaeacians. But Poseidon stirred up the sea and sent a huge wave to crash the raft. "Ah me! What misfortune this is! Would that I had perished with Achilles in Troy. At least that would have been a good death," wept Odysseus. The raft was torn apart but Leucothoe[56], the White Goddess took pity on him and offered her veil of protection. He swam around for four days wearing nothing but the veil of protection and reached the rocky shores of the Phoeacians. The land was rough and Odysseus wandered through thick forests. He got under a wild olive bush to shield himself from the scorching sun. He tore down branches from the tree to cover his nakedness and slept upon the dried leaves waiting for whatever fate might throw his way.

CHAPTER FORTY-NINE

THE PRINCESS OF PHAEACIA

"'I never yet saw any one so beautiful, neither man nor woman, and am lost in admiration as I behold you. I can only compare you to a young palm tree which I saw when I was at Delos growing near the altar of Apollo-'" Homer, *Odyssey* Book VI [518]

The Phaeacians had once been neighbours to the Cyclopes and ravaged other lands. The Cyclopes took advantage of their friendship and attacked them. King Nausithous warred against the monsters and sent them far into their own island. He built a new city with walls for protection. He built temples to the gods and ruled his people wisely. But that was a long time ago and Nausithous was now dead and gone to Hades. The land was ruled by his son Alcinous, who was his peer in counsel and strength. King Alcinous had a beautiful daughter named Nausicaa. The princess was asleep in her ornately decorated chamber with her two maids. Goddess Athena went to Nausicaa and sent a dream to the sleeping princess. She inspired the idea of going out to the washing pools and washing her beautiful clothes.

At dawn, Nausicaa woke up and donned her purple robe. She went straight to her mother, Queen Arete, who sat upon the hearth with her maids, spinning purple sea-dyed yarn. She told her mother about her dream and asked her father for wagons and horses to go to the washing pools. He immediately ordered the servants to fetch wagons and mules. Nausicaa brought out all the dirty linen and loaded them in a side cart. Her mother filled a box with bread, cheese, grilled meats, delicacies and fine red wine. She also gave Nausicaa a golden flask of olive oil so that the princess and her maids could anoint themselves after bathing. Nausicaa took the whip and lashed the mules. Some of the maids accompanied her while the others followed on foot.

They reached the lovely river and the washing pools were brimming with crystal-clear water. They unharnessed the mules and left them to eat fresh grass. The maids began washing the clothes. Once they were rinsed, the maids spread them over the rocks upon the seashore to dry. Next, after bathing and anointing themselves with olive oil, Nausicaa and the maids ate the meal. They started playing with a ball while Nausicaa sang and kept the score. Nausicaa was tall and majestic just like the goddess Artemis. Odysseus was sleeping behind the wild olive bushes and he was woken up by their screams of joy. He crept out of the bushes and leapt towards them hoping they would provide him food. He was grimy, dirty and naked except for a branch of olive leaves. The girls shrieked in terror and ran away; all except Nausicaa.

Odysseus fell upon his feet and spoke to her; "Princess, I come to you for help. Are you some goddess or nymph or a mortal woman? Never have I set my eyes on such a majestic woman as you. I am filled with awe when I look at you. I dare not clasp your knees for that might offend you. Pity me and give me some rags to cover myself. Please direct me to town. And may the gods bless you with a fine husband and a prosperous home since there is nothing in this world better than a man and his wife keeping home in joy and their reputation spreading far and wide."

"Sir," said the beautiful Nausicaa, "your manners show that you are not a savage. Some god has given you misfortune and now that you have come to our country, I will show you the way to town. I am the daughter of mighty Alcinous, king of the Phaeacian people." She ordered her maids to wash Odysseus and anoint him with olive oil. They brought him a tunic and a cloak to wear. Nausicaa gave him food and while he ate, she wished that the stranger might stay with her forever as her husband. Then she said, "Come, sir, our city is always crowded and I cannot accompany you because I wish to avoid gossip. You must enter the path that runs by a fine poplar wood. The path leads straight to the palace. Cross the gates and enter the courtyard. Go straight to the throne hall and speak to my mother who sits by the hearth and spins purple wool." Nausicaa left after giving him directions to her father's palace.

The goddess Athena enveloped Odysseus in a thick mist and he went unnoticed till he reached the throne hall of Alcinous' palace. Odysseus marvelled at the splendid harbour on the way and admired the stout ships for the Phaeacians were skilled sailors of the time. Odysseus was taken aback by the luxury of the palace. The threshold was of bronze. So were the walls and the high-vaulted roofs and battlements. Enamel friezes adorned the walls. The doors were made of solid gold and the doorposts of silver. On either side of the main entrance stood Hephaestus' silver and gold dogs that the god had gifted Alcinous. Tall chairs stood around the throne hall in a row and to the side was a tapestry-covered area reserved for the women. This was where Queen Arete sat with her maids and wove purple wool. Many noble Phaeacians sat on the chairs and enjoyed the choicest food. Golden statues of young men and women holding blazing torches adorned the pillars. There was a large garden outside with fruit orchards and vineyards. Springs of clear water were skillfully diverted to run around the plantations and orchards.

Odysseus went straight to Queen Arete and said, "Queen Arete, I come to you as a suppliant. May the gods grant you, your husband and children a long life and prosperity. But for me, please arrange an escort to sail with me back to my own country for I have traversed much misfortune." King Alcinous made Odysseus sit on a tall polished chair and ordered the servants to bring meat and bread. A maid brought water in a golden flask and poured it over a silver bowl so that he may wash his hands. She drew a wooden table and an upper servant brought a basket filled with the choicest slices of hot crisp bread. Another servant brought a bowl of cheese and meat. Odysseus ate his fill. Alcinous mixed a bowl with wine and they made libations to Zeus. Then they drank their fill.

Alcinous had observed the way Odysseus reached his hearth surrounded by mist. So he spoke first once Odysseus had finished eating. "Sir, surely you must be an immortal god come down from Olympus because none of us saw you enter the palace. If that is the case, then I wonder why as many deities have appeared before in their original forms and we have sacrificed to them. If you are an ordinary traveller, why the concealment? Pray, enlighten us," said Alcinous.

"King Alcinous, I have neither the form nor the wisdom of the gods. I am a wretch who has suffered much. My heart is sick with grief but my stomach forces me to eat my fill. Once I settle down in my own home and hearth, I will be content," said Odysseus. But Queen Arete had a sharp eye. She noticed that the stranger wore the cloak and tunic she had made. She spoke with a gleaming eye, "Sir, who are you? Where do you come from? And who gave you these clothes?" The shrewd Odysseus told her his adventures on Ogygia and how Calypso had offered to make him immortal. He told her how Nausicaa had helped him once he reached their island and offered him clothing. However, he did not reveal his name or his homeland.

"My friend, I am indeed happy that Zeus, Athena and Poseidon have brought you to us. I wish that a man like you could have my daughter and become my son-in-law. I would give you a house and riches. That is only if you are willing to stay. We Phaeacians never force anyone against their will. And to comfort you, I promise to give you a ship and a crew. They will sail you safely while you sleep on board and leave you wherever you direct them to go. You shall be the judge of my sailors as they have surpassed many in their skill," said Alcinous in delight. He secretly wished that the stranger would marry his daughter and stay there forever.

At dawn, Alcinous called his council and announced games in honour of the stranger. He invited the divinely inspired minstrel Demodocus to sing in the preceding feast and entertain them with the tales of heroes. Alcinous sacrificed a dozen sheep, eight white-tusked boars and two oxen. Demodocus was given the king's favourite seat and offered the best portions first. He stringed his harp and sang the adventures of Achilles and Odysseus. When the hero heard tales of his suffering, he hid his face behind his purple tunic and wept. Alcinous noticed this and asked them to start the games. Laodamus, the son of Alcinous excelled at all events. When it was time to throw the discus, he provoked Odysseus. The hero picked up the largest stone discus and threw it with one mighty swing. The stone sang as it swept past and landed far from the stones of others. Alcinous appreciated him and launched a huge ship for him. He ordered fifty-two young men to sail with Odysseus.

Demodocus sang again to entertain the guests. This time he sang of Aphrodite and Ares and how Hephaestus caught them in his net-like contraption. Then he started singing about the Wooden Horse of Troy. Odysseus wept again and Alcinous stopped the minstrel in mid-song. He looked to Odysseus and asked, "Hear me good captains and counsellors, I ask this to our guest in front of you so that you may be the witness to what he has to say. Come, sir, it is time to speak out. Tell us your name and your homeland. Tell us about your wanderings." Odysseus could hide no further and he told them everything - his name and parentage, his adventures at Troy, the misfortune with the Cyclopes, Circe and the journey to the Underworld, Scylla and Charybdis and finally his bewitchment by Calypso and how he had been saved by Nausicaa.

Alcinous heard all this and his heart melted for his guest. He rose and said, "Odysseus, now that you have reached my house, you shall eat and drink your fill. And as promised, I will see to it that you reach Ithaca safely. Each of my captains and counsellors will offer you a large tripod and a cauldron as a parting gift. I myself will give you rich gifts and see you off at dawn." Odysseus was very pleased and thanked his host. The next day, Alcinous got up early before dawn and went into the ship that he had launched for his guest. He personally checked all the rigging and the trimming of each sail. He also sacrificed a bull to Zeus for safe passage. Every captain and counsellor brought their tripod and cauldron and loaded them in the ship's hold. Queen Arete presented Odysseus with a newly woven cloak and tunic. She also placed a cask of wine and a box of corn, bread and meats. The servants spread a soft rug and a linen sheet on board and Odysseus slept on it. The skilled Phaeacians launched the ship and she cut across the waves like a four-horse chariot.

The ship reached Ithaca faster than any other ship and dropped anchor in the cavern of Phorcys. This cavern was sacred to the nymphs and shaded from the sun. The sailors lifted the sleeping Odysseus and left him under an olive tree. They also left all his gifts and sailed back silently. Poseidon watched everything silently and grumbled. He wanted to teach the Phaeacians a lesson for giving people safe passage home. With the permission of Zeus, he wrecked the ship as it entered Alcinous harbour. Then he turned her into a rock. Alcinous watched this and remembered an old prophecy. He knew that Poseidon would be angry at sailing people and also bury his city under a mountain. He hurriedly went out and sacrificed twelve bulls to Poseidon. But the Earth-shaker was not appeased. Anyway, Odysseus reached home safely but he still had a lot of work to do. And Vengeance was waiting at his threshold, sharpening her sword.

CHAPTER FIFTY

THE LOYAL SWINEHERD AND THE MAN IN DISGUISE

"'. . . go where I may I shall never find so good a master, not even if I were to go home to my mother and father where I was bred and born. . . it is the loss of Ulysses that grieves me most; I cannot speak of him without reverence though he is here no longer, for he was very fond of me that wherever he may be I shall always honour his memory.'" Homer, *Odyssey* Book XIV [622]

Odysseus woke up and trembled to find himself in another land. He did not recognize his own homeland. He looked around and found his gifts. Athena appeared before him and said, "Odysseus, son of Laertes, this is your own Ithaca. Now you must hide your treasures in this cavern and go forward to claim your home for more troubles await you."

"Goddess, my companion and guardian, I know you have been watching over me all along. Tell me truly, what bad luck waits at home for me?" asked Odysseus.

"Your home has been ruined these three years by suitors who have come to claim your wife's hand in marriage. They spend their time making wedding presents for your wife and holding grand feasts. They have slaughtered all your cattle and ruined your home. However, your wife has been tricking them and lamenting for you all these years. Your son, Telemachus has left to ask your whereabouts to Nestor. He is now with Menelaus while the suitors are planning an ambush to kill him on his way home. Do not worry. I will bring your son home safely. Meanwhile, let me disguise you. You must stay with your swineherd till your son meets you," advised the goddess. She took away his fine golden hair and withered the flesh in his body. She dressed him in a rough deerskin and the disguise was so good that Odysseus could not recognise himself.

Odysseus walked along the rough wooded country path and reached the cottage of his swineherd. Athena had told him that the swineherd was the most loyal of all his servants. He found the man sitting in front of his thatched cottage which was surrounded by fenced enclosures for the pigs. There were only fifty pigs in each stye and this was because the suitors had slaughtered all the rest. There were four hounds lying at his feet. His name was Eumaeus and he tied the dogs when he saw an old man approaching him. Odysseus introduced himself as a Cretan warrior lost at sea and Eumaeus made him welcome. He offered the stranger the servants' pork and made a bed from twigs and rushes. He also spoke valiantly of his master and hoped he would return. Odysseus was glad to hear his servant speak so highly of him.

The goddess Athena went to Sparta to fetch Telemachus. Athena of the flashing eyes had already appeared to him in the guise of Mentes, the chieftain of the seafaring Taphians and asked him to visit Nestor and Menelaus. Nestor was the wisest of all and he would share the whereabouts of Odysseus. Menelaus was the last to return back to Greece from Troy and he must have seen or heard about Odysseus. Nestor had advised Telemachus: "Heed my warning, son of Odysseus! Do not stay too long or too far from home nor leave your wealth unguarded among brutes." He had also given his best chariot and an escort to conduct Telemachus safely to Lacedaemon (Sparta) where Menelaus lived.

Menelaus was celebrating the wedding of his daughter when Telemachus reached the rolling hills of Lacedaemon. His beautiful daughter Hermione was to marry Neoptolemus, the son of Achilles. Menelaus and Achilles had struck the deal during the Trojan War. Fair-haired Helen sat down at her loom while her husband sat on his throne and listened to the tales of Telemachus. Menelaus spoke of his adventures in Egypt on his way home. He also spoke proudly of the tactics of Odysseus. Menelaus entertained Telemachus with grand feasts, songs and sports. Helen and the maids offered him soft cloaks and tunics. It was at this place that golden-haired Athena arrived. She saw Telemachus sleeping and appeared to him in his dream. She said, "Telemachus, it is wrong of you to linger around in luxury while the suitors storm your house. Your mother's father and brothers are pressing her to marry Eurymachus. Some of these suitors have planned to ambush you on the strait of Samos before you reach Ithaca. Steer your ship clear of Samos and when you reach home, visit your loyal swineherd first."

Telemachus woke his host at dawn and asked permission to return home. Menelaus ordered his slaves to prepare a mighty feast for his guest. He also went to his treasure chamber with Helen and picked the choicest gifts for Telemachus. First of all, he chose a two-handled cup of solid gold and a silver mixing bowl made by Hepahestus. Helen opened her chest of dresses and picked an elaborately woven gown that glittered like stars. She had made the dress herself and gave it to Telemachus as a gift to his bride to wear on their wedding day. With these on board his ship, Telemachus cast off anchor and Athena sent him a strong wind that drove him past Samos safely. He took his bronze spear and walked towards the hut of Eumaeus as soon as the ship reached Ithaca.

Eumaeus, the swineherd, was overjoyed to see Telemachus enter his hut. "You are back, Telemachus, light of my eyes! I thought I would never see you again when you went out to see Nestor," he said in joy. Telemachus saw Odysseus who was disguised as a beggar. Eumaeus made them sit on a fleece spread over brushwood and offered them meat and wine in olive wood bowls. After the meal, Telemachus stepped out to go to the palace when Athena appeared to Odysseus and changed him back. Telemachus marvelled at the transformation and said, "Stranger, how you have changed! Surely you are a god come down from Olympus. Be gracious to us and we will make you sacrifices and offerings of gold."

"I am no god," said Odysseus, "I am no immortal but your mortal father. I am that man for whom you have endured so much." Odysseus embraced his son and kissed him. Telemachus was surprised and overjoyed at the same time. "Tell me son, and tell me truly, who are these suitors? What have they been doing to my home? What has happened to Penelope?" asked Odysseus.

"Dearest father, these suitors have been perplexing mother and ruining your home for as long as I can remember. There are not just ten or twenty but hundreds of them. They have also brought their slaves, upper servants, grooms, carvers, heralds and minstrels to entertain them. They begin their day by slaughtering your cattle and enjoying lavish feasts while listening to their minstrels. Then they compete against each other in offering wedding presents to mother. She neither encourages them nor rejects them. Then they conduct games and amuse themselves by hunting your game. They have diminished your special wine reserves and your choicest cattle," said Telemachus distraught. Odysseus thought long and hard. Then the Versatile Man sprang up. He shared his plan with Telemachus.

"Listen, son, and listen well. If you are truly of my blood, tell no one of my arrival, not even your mother or your grandfather. These suitors must face their doom from my hand. Go to the palace tomorrow and take all the weapons from the throne room and hide them. But leave a couple of swords, spears and shields for us to grab when the time comes. I'll come to the palace later disguised as a beggar and you must not aid me when the suitors insult or even throw me out. Once we are inside, we must learn the attitude of the maids for some of them may help the suitors. The servants must also be judged on their loyalty," said Odysseus. Telemachus agreed and when Aurora, the rosy-fingered goddess of dawn appeared on the east, he left for the palace.

CHAPTER FIFTY-ONE

THE BOW OF IPHITUS

"He took an arrow that was lying upon the table-for those which the Achaeans were so shortly about to taste were all inside the quiver-he laid it on the centre-piece of the bow, and drew the notch of the arrow and the string toward him, still seated on his seat. When he had taken aim he let fly, and his arrow pierced every one of the handle-holes of the axes from the first onwards till it had gone right through them, and into the outer courtyard." Homer, *Odyssey* [724-25]

The suitors eagerly awaited news of Telemachus' death. They were indeed surprised to see him walk into the throne hall, his eyes gleaming with confidence and his spear freshly sharpened. Once he went to the upper chamber to greet his mother, Eurymachus and Antinous got talking. These two were the wealthiest suitors of all and vied with each other to get Penelope's hand. "Damn Telemachus! How did he escape the ambush? Some god must have brought him home. As long as he lives, Penelope will not consent to marry any one of us. The people have his respect. He must be killed if we are to rule Ithaca," said Eurymachus.

"We must kill him on his way to town or on the road. Then we could divide his estates among us. But let the man who marries Penelope keep the palace," said Antinous.

"My friends, it is a horrible thing to spill the blood of princes," said Amphinomus, another suitor. He was a virtuous man and Penelope admired his just speeches. "Let us learn the gods' will and act likewise," he said and moved away from the conspirators. Penelope had overheard them all. She stormed from the queen's chamber and stood behind a pillar. She covered her beautiful face with a shining veil and spoke, "You arrogant men! You plan to spill the blood of a man's son - a man who has saved your people from enemies and rescued you on the battlefield. How can you do this?"

"Penelope, gentle daughter of Icarius[57], have no fear. No one will harm Telemachus and I assure this on my honour," said Eurymachus but his mind was already plotting against Telemachus. Penelope wept and said, "You men are not wooing me according to the customs of my land. Honourable men courting a woman of noble birth bring their own provisions and magnificent gifts for the woman, instead of eating up other people's property."

"Queen Penelope, take as many gifts as you like from us. But none of us will budge until you have married the best among us, whoever he may be," said Antinous and all applauded him. All the suitors commanded their servants to bring the best gift they could for Penelope. Antinous brought a magnificent dress exquisitely embroidered. It had twelve gold brooch pin-fasteners. Eurymachus immediately brought a stunning necklace of gold and amber beads that shone like the sun. Eurydamas gave a set of three-tiered earrings and Pisander a necklace that glittered like stars. Everyone brought her a beautiful gift.

Penelope did not wait to see the gifts. She had merely spoken to insult the suitors. She went back to her chamber and shut her doors. Her maid brought all the gifts behind her. The poor queen fell on her bed and wept herself to sleep. Penelope had been tormented by the suitors for so long that she had come up with a plan. Once when Eurymachus had forced her to make a decision, she said she could not marry before making a funeral shroud for Laertes, the father of Odysseus. The man was dying and the shroud must be made. Every day, she sat at her loom weaving the most exquisite shroud one could think of. But at night, unknown to all, she unwove the linen. She had kept at it for three years till Melantho, a slave, discovered her trickery and revealed it to the suitors. But at her heart's core, she missed her husband and sincerely hoped that he would return and teach them all a lesson.

Meanwhile, the other suitors were outside throwing the javelin and the discus. Medon, the herald announced the time for supper and they slaughtered a dozen full-grown sheep, several pigs and a heifer for their feast. Medon loved Odysseus dearly and served the suitors against his will. Then they sat themselves down on the cushions in the great dining hall. The upper servants rushed around with water bowls, mixing bowls, wine casks, bread baskets and cheese platters. The carvers offered them their favourite portions of meat while the minstrels sang. While this was going on, Athena once again changed the appearance of Odysseus. Eumaeus brought him to the palace. Odysseus recognized his magnificent palace with its colossal battlements, chambers upon chambers constructed out of solid stone, courtyards of the finest marble and doors of wrought gold. Argus, Odysseus' faithful hound lay abandoned among the garbage. The hero had bred him and the suitors had taken him out for hunting. But now Argus was too old and the suitors had thrown him out with garbage. The loyal beast recognised his master and yelped. Having waited for twenty years to see his master, Argus died soon enough. Odysseus brushed off a tear and walked towards the main gates.

Telemachus saw Eumaeus bring the wretched old beggar leaning on a stick, clothed in filthy rags. He called his servant and said, "Take this meat and offer it to the stranger. Tell him to beg scraps from each suitor in turn." The servant obeyed and Odysseus begged scraps from each suitor. All of them gave him something, all except the haughty Antinous. "Haven't we had enough of beggars and vagrants licking our plates? Why must there be a curse on our supper? Stand clear of the table or I will have to deal you with my sword!" Antinous picked up a stool and threw it at Odysseus. It hit him on the shoulder but Odysseus did not filch. Penelope was sitting behind her woven curtain on her loom while she watched the whole scene. "I hope Apollo strikes you as you struck the poor beggar!" she retorted.

The suitors enjoyed a hearty supper and then called out Irus. This man was a beggar known for his strength and he ran errands for the suitors. Antinous called out to Odysseus, "Beggar, let's see how you fight. I'll offer you a sheep's stomach stuffed with meat if you can take out Irus!" Both of them jumped into the boxing ring that the suitors had constructed on Odysseus' terrace. Irus aimed a blow at Odysseus' shoulder but the hero evaded it and landed an enormous punch on Irus' ear. He smashed the bone and

Irus fell down grimacing in pain while a trickle of blood streamed out of his ear. The suitors cheered. Amphinomus spoke to the beggar, "My friend, let's drink to your health! You are having a tough time but may you reach home safely!" Odysseus said, "Amphinomus, I recognise you. Let me warn you, my friend. The master of this house will soon return and there will be much blood spilt soon. Return to your home while you can." Amphinomus walked away with a heavy heart but fate had already marked him for death.

Penelope ordered her nurse Eurycleia to prepare a bath and a bed for the beggar. Old Eurycleia drew warm water in a tub. As Odysseus undressed, she noticed a familiar scar on his thigh. Eurycleia had practically raised Odysseus and recognised him at once. Odysseus shut her mouth and said, "Not a word, woman! I'm here to exact vengeance. Hold your tongue and tell no one of my arrival." Eurycleia happily accepted and walked away in joy. Towards dusk, Penelope called in an archery contest. She went down to the storeroom and got Odysseus' massive bow from its shining case. This was gifted to Odysseus by the great hero Iphitus. No one except the two of them could string it. Penelope brought twelve axes and asked Telemachus to dig a trench and plant the axes along. She announced that she would marry the man who would shoot his arrow through all the twelve axes. She had had enough. Telemachus took the bow and said, "Look here, fine suitors! This is the most exquisite piece of weaponry ever made. Let me try first and if I win, at least I will be proud enough to earn my father's bow." He tried to string it thrice and failed. Then he handed it over to the others. Many of them had delicate hands and could not even pull back the string.

Telemachus had already asked his servants to lock the door of the great hall. The bow came to Eurymachus. He warmed the bow in fire but failed to string it. Then he cried, "Damn this bow! Anyway, there are plenty of worthy maidens in Ithaca for me to marry. What grieves me most is that this proves us weaklings before the strength of Odysseus!" Antinous called for a wine break. While the suitors were drinking mellow wine, Odysseus asked if he could have a try. The suitors were enraged. "Miserable wretch! How dare you? Do you think for one moment that we would let you try Odysseus' bow? This is such an insult to us!" yelled Antinous.

"Antinous! It is not common decency to be so rude to Telemachus' guests! Do you imagine that the stranger will string the bow and carry me to his home? Are you afraid of a little competition?" said the enraged Penelope.

"Penelope, wise queen, do not imagine that this man will win your hand. We hope that the people of Ithaca will not humiliate us if he does string the bow. Our honour has to be preserved," said Eurymachus.

"Eurymachus! What honour is there in men who destroy a great man's household? If you all had honour, you would have brought your own provisions while you wooed me. Our guest may be a beggar but he is of noble birth. If he does succeed, I will give him a fine cloak and a tunic, a sharp javelin, a two-edged sword and sandals for his feet," said Penelope.

"Mother! It is my right to give my father's bow to whoever I wish. I am the master of this house and this man is my guest," said Telemachus. The bow was brought to Odysseus and he picked it up with pride. He bent the string at both ends with a critic's eye. He plucked the string and it sang like a lyre. He took the bronze-tipped arrow from the table and notched it against the bow. There was a flash of lightning and a clap of thunder at that moment and

Odysseus was joyful to receive the sign of Zeus. He fired the arrow and it struck all twelve axes. Then he nodded silently and Telemachus locked the doors. He also armed himself with his sword and shield. At that instant, Nemesis[58] marched into the hall and blew upon the bugle of death.

CHAPTER FIFTY-TWO

THE HALL OF BLOOD

"'Begin,' said he, 'to remove the dead, and make the women help you. Then, get sponges and clean water to swill down the tables and seats. When you have thoroughly cleansed the whole cloisters, take the women into the space between the domed room and the wall of the outer court, and run them through with your swords till they are quite dead, and have forgotten all about love and the way in which they used to lie in secret with the suitors.'" Homer, *Odyssey* Book XXII [736-37]

Odysseus threw off his rags and jumped upon a stool, stringing his bow and pouring all the bronze-tipped arrows at his feet. He threw off the carved quiver and cried, "Now begins the contest that seals your fate!" He aimed at Antinous and shot him in the neck. Antinous dropped his wine goblet and fell flat upon the ground, blood gushing from his nostrils. The suitors were horrified and started running around for dear life. "You fools!" roared Odysseus, "You never thought you'd see me back from Troy. So you ruined my household, raped my maids and wooed my wife. Nemesis has sealed your fates!" Eurymachus was the only one to speak out. He said, "Odysseus, if you really are who you say you are, then believe me. Antinous was the one responsible for all the evils here - he wanted to become king of Ithaca. He was the one who planned to kill your son. But he has been killed. So spare us and we will repay you with bronze cauldrons and a contribution of twenty oxen each."

Vengeful Odysseus did not listen to a word. The suitors turned the tables and unsheathed their swords. They decided to fight him as best they could. Eurymachus drew his keen sword of bronze and rushed at Odysseus. But the Versatile Man shot a quick arrow that pierced through Eurymachus' liver. He dropped his sword and doubled over the table upsetting the wine goblet and meat basket. Amphinomus was next but Telemachus struck him from behind. Telemachus was a little bit afraid to pull out his spear from Amphinomus' body. So he ran and stood behind his father. Telemachus went out for more weapons and brought four shields, eight bronze spears and four bronze helmets with plumes. They armed themselves while the cowherd and the swineherd Eumaeus also joined them. Odysseus shot every suitor till his arrows ran out. Then he grasped his two bronze spears. He looked like the valiant Ares storming into the battlefield.

Melanthius, one of the servants of Odysseus, opened the trapdoor to the armoury and brought weapons for the suitors. Telemachus had left the door unfastened in a hurry and the traitor grasped his opportunity. Eumaeus reported this to Odysseus who commanded thus; "Seize the traitor! Bind his hands and feet, then carry him to the roof and run a noose around his body. Hang him from the roof so that he may endure agony for a long time before dying." Eumaeus and the cowherd followed his orders and Melanthius faced his fate. The suitors, who by this time had armed themselves again, began throwing spears at Odysseus and Telemachus. But Athena diverted the spears away from the hero and his son. But Odysseus and his team threw their spears and killed Demoptolemus, Euryades, Elatus and Pisander. Odysseus and his team fell upon the suitors like vultures bearing down upon corpses. The smooth marmoreal throne hall was now wet with blood, brains and innards. The columns and pillars of bronze were dripping with gore and filth.

The minstrel Phemius who was forced to sing by the suitors tried to plead for his life. He grasped Odysseus' knees and said, "Most noble Odysseus, I beseech you, please have mercy on me and spare my life. It is not heroic to kill a bard who sings for gods and men. Your own son will tell you that I was forced to sing and serve by the suitors." Telemachus immediately rushed to his father's side and said, "Yes father, this man is guiltless. Medon too, for he remains your faithful herald." Odysseus spared them both and said, "Fear not, for you shall come to no harm. Keep away from the slaughter while we finish our work." The two of them ran into the courtyard in fear and gratitude.

Next, Odysseus summoned his nurse Euryclea. The old woman came from the women's chambers and was horrified to see Odysseus standing among the corpses of his enemies, covered in gore and filth much like a lion that has just devoured an ox. "Old woman!" said Odysseus, "now tell me, which of the maids in the house have misconducted themselves and which are innocent."

"Odysseus, my son, I will tell you the truth. There are fifty maids in the household. Of these, twelve have misbehaved despite my warnings and the commands of your wife Penelope. Let me go and tell Penelope of your arrival so that she may rejoice. Let's not keep her waiting for long," said Euryclea.

"Do not wake her yet. But ask the twelve women to come to me," commanded Odysseus. Then he turned to Telemachus and Eumaeus and said, "Move the corpses and make the women clean the halls. Fetch sponges and clean water. Let them wipe every seat and table. Every column and every pillar must be washed. Once they have finished their task, kill them with your swords for that will teach them a lesson for sleeping with the suitors," said Odysseus.

The maids came down from their cloisters, weeping and wailing for what lay ahead. They carried the corpses and propped them outside. They cleaned everything thoroughly while Telemachus and the servants shovelled up the gore and filth from the floor. Once the entire palace was clean, Telemachus and the others marched the women into the narrow space between the wall of the gatehouse and the courtyard so that they could not escape. "These maids have disobeyed my mother and slept with the suitors. They have disclosed the locations of the armoury, the treasury and the granary to them. These traitors deserve the worst of deaths," said Telemachus. So instead of stabbing them, he brought out a ship's cable and made twelve nooses. He hanged all the women and they died a most miserable death, their feet twitching and writhing. They brought down Melanthius from the roof to the courtyard. They cut off his nose and ears, cut open his stomach and pulled out his innards and gave them to the dogs to eat. Then they chopped off his hands and feet.

Once Odysseus was completely satisfied with his vengeance and killed every one of the suitors, he called Euryclea. "Light a fire and bring me some sulphur to cleanse the pollution. Bring me a cloak and tunic," he said. Odysseus purified all the cloisters, halls and chambers with smoke and sulphur. Then he washed himself and donned the clean cloak and tunic. By this time, all his faithful servants and maids rushed around him, embracing him and kissing him in joy. He felt happy to be home again and remembered what Ithaca truly felt like.

CHAPTER FIFTY-THREE

The Olive Bed and the Country Home

"'First observe this scar,' answered Ulysses, 'which I got from a boar's tusk when I was hunting on Mt. Parnassus. . . Furthermore, I will point out to the trees in the vineyard which you gave me. . . You gave me thirteen pear trees, ten apple trees and forty fig trees; you also said you would give me fifty rows of vines; there was corn planted between each row, and they yield grapes of every kind when the heat of heaven has been laid heavy upon them.'" Homer, *Odyssey* Book XXIV [757]

Old Euryclea ran upstairs in joy to tell her mistress that Odysseus was home. She felt that her youth had come back to her as she bounded into Penelope's chamber. The queen was asleep upon wet pillows as she had cried herself to sleep. "Wake up Penelope, wake up! Now is not the time to sleep! Odysseus is home again and he has killed all the suitors who troubled you," said Euryclea as she woke Penelope up. Penelope did not believe her nurse and thought that the old woman had gone mad. Nevertheless, she came downstairs in search of her son. She entered the throne hall and sat down near the hearth facing Odysseus. She did not speak. Telemachus was the one to break the silence.

"Mother, you are so cold and hard! How can you keep away from father? No other woman will be silent when her husband returns home after twenty years but your heart has always been hard," said Telemachus.

"My son," said Penelope, "I am astounded as I cannot find words to speak! If this is indeed Odysseus, we shall get to know each other gradually through certain secrets that we alone know."

"Let your mother test me any way she likes," said Odysseus, "Meanwhile, we must be ready to face the wrath of the suitors' kin. First, let us get dressed and ask Phemius to perform his lyre. If anyone from outside sees the palace, they must think we are celebrating a wedding. Then we will retreat into the woods to my country house. There we will decide what to do." Odysseus washed and anointed himself with olive oil. He wore his best tunic embroidered with gold. He looked like a god as he sat down to supper. It was during the meal that Penelope put him to her test.

"Nurse, I will be sleeping alone tonight. Bring Odysseus' bed outside our chamber and put bedding upon it with fleeces, woollen coverlets and soft blankets," said Penelope as she stood up after supper.

"Wife, you may sleep where you like. But tell me, and tell me true, who has dismantled my bed? There is no mortal alive who can dismantle my bed for I made it with my own hands. When I built my chamber, there was a young olive growing in the centre and its trunk was as large as a bearing post. I built my chamber around it with stone. Then I chopped off the topmost boughs and left only the trunk. I dressed this carefully with my carpentry and made it into a bedpost. I inlaid it with gold and silver and spread crimson leather in the centre. So how is it, that it can be moved?" said Odysseus. When she heard this, Penelope almost fainted with joy. She ran to him, weeping, and threw her arms around his neck. Then she said, "Do not be angry with me, dear Odysseus. I was afraid that some imposter might come here and deceive me. Now, however, you have convinced me by explaining the details about our bed which no other mortal knows. I mistrust you no longer. I only weep because we have been away and the gods have denied us the pleasure of spending our youth together and of growing old together." Odysseus' heart melted in happiness and he thanked the gods for being blessed with such a faithful wife.

Odysseus told his wife all his adventures - starting with the Cicons and ending with the Phaeacians. Penelope listened in delight but she knew something was bothering him. She asked him what it was and he said, "Wife, I have to announce the death of the suitors. Lock yourself in your chambers and do not come out till the matter is settled. I am going to our country home to see my old father Laertes. As for the cattle that the suitors had eaten, I will demand the Achaeans to fill my yard." At sunrise, he woke up and donned his armour. He also told Telemachus and Eumaeus to put on their armour too. Then they opened the gates and walked into town. It was still dark and the mystic Athena concealed their shadowy forms.

Odysseus and the others walked along through the woods till they reached the well-tilled farms of Laertes.

There were separate enclosures for the sheep, pigs and cows. Laertes had put much labour into his prized orchards and vineyards. Slaves were busy fencing his vineyard and carrying pails of fresh cream from the dairy. Odysseus found Laertes in the vineyard hoeing a vine. He had on a dirty patched shirt and leather thongs. Laertes did not believe that it was indeed his son who was standing near him. Odysseus showed him the scar on his thigh. Then he named every tree in the orchard. Laertes threw his arms around his son and Odysseus had to carry him as his knees gave out. Laertes called his servants to prepare a feast in honour of his son's return.

While the happy group was feasting, news of the suitors spread about town. People heard of it and came to Odysseus' palace. The kinsmen of the dead came and collected the corpses. Those who remained were put on board fishing vessels to be delivered to their kinsmen. Then they gathered before Odysseus' palace and Eupeithes led the riot. He was in grief for his dead son Antinous. Odysseus, Telemachus and Eumaeus were just returning from their country home. Laertes was also with them. They drew their swords and rushed at the mob. Laertes aimed his spear at Eupeithes' bronze helmet and threw his spear in the name of Athena. The spear went clean through the helmet and Eupeithes went down straight to the halls of Hades.

The clash would have continued if not for a magnificent eagle that flew from the heavens and alighted upon the field. Then it transformed into a handsome woman; tall, strong and shining with courage. She held a gold spear and the sacred aegis of Zeus with the gorgon Medusa's head on it. It was Athena, the blue-eyed goddess of wisdom and war from Mt. Olympus. She cried, "Men of Ithaca, halt this raging strife! Settle the matter at once without bloodshed!" The men were horrified and stood frozen. Odysseus and the others settled matters peacefully with each other and Athena went back to Mt. Olympus. Odysseus ruled Ithaca peacefully for many years and he became known far and wide for his intelligence and prudence as much for his valour and strength. If Achilles had died a warrior's death in battle, Odysseus achieved higher fame by returning home to his family. For a man's home is his strength and his family is his true power.

Glossary

1. The Deluge - the flood summoned by Zeus to destroy the world, thereby ridding it of evil-minded men and making way for new creations to emerge. Apparently, Zeus was dissatisfied with the Bronze Age where people started killing their own fathers, mothers and kin. The Bronze Age was marked by corruption, murder, vengeance, deception and falsehood. Zeus was angered by Lycaon, King of Babylonia. When Zeus descended upon Earth in disguise, everyone recognised him and bowed in respect. Lycaon decided to test Zeus to find out if he was really a god. So he captured a slave from prison, slit his throat and roasted his innards. He served these to Zeus. After the feast, Lycaon planned on murdering Zeus to check his immortality. Zeus changed Lycaon and his kin to wolves. Then he opened the heavens and summoned the deluge. He commanded Poseidon to join all rivers and seas. The whole world was swept by the seas. Only mermaids and sea creatures survived the deluge.

2. Deucalion and Pyrrha - the first man and woman created by Zeus. After the deluge ebbed back into the sea and the rivers separated, the land became fertile. Deucalion was the son of Prometheus. Young Deucalion and his wife Pyrrha survived the deluge and made it to the city of Phocis in a tiny boat. They came to the shrine of Themis and prayed for guidance. Themis appeared in a vision and said, "Scatter your mother's bones." These 'bones' were stones and he threw them on the fertile earth. Those thrown by Deucalion became men and

those by Pyrrha became women.

3. Delphi - an ancient city sacred to Apollo, the god of music, poetry and medicine. This city held a shrine to Apollo where the famous Oracle of Delphi (also called Pythia) gave out prophecies to those who sought the god's advice. Herodotus, in his *Histories,* records various monarchs who donated magnanimously to the shrine before going to war.

4. Erichthonius - the son of Athena and Hephaestos. Athena was a virgin goddess of war and she had taken a vow of celibacy. However, during the Trojan War, she became close with Hephaestos who forged weapons for her heroes. Hephaestos had recently discovered his wife Aphrodite's lust for Ares. The sudden presence of the radiant Athena awoke lust in him and he decided to rape her. He forced her but she shoved him off with her immeasurable strength. But he had already sprayed his seed all over her. Disgusted, she wiped herself and threw the seed from Mt. Olympus over the earth. The seed landed on the earth's surface and transformed into a monstrous baby, half-human and half-monster.

5. Nyctimene - princess of Lesbos, daughter of King Epopeus. Ovid states that she defiled her father's bed, meaning she seduced her own father much like Myrrha. But she repented her sin and Athena took pity on her. Athena changed Nyctimene into an owl and took the bird as her sacred symbol.

6. Chiron - the centaur who raises heroes and sends them on their quests. Apollo himself taught him archery, medicine, music, hunting, gymnastics and prophecy. Hence, he was the wisest of the centaurs. He raised Achilles, Jason and Aesculapius.

7. Europa - daughter of Agenor, heir to Poseidon; seduced

by Zeus and gave birth to Minos, King of Crete. Zeus abducted her in the form of a beautiful white bull.

8. Tiresias - a divine seer, also known as the Prophet of Thebes; once he struck a pair of mating snakes and was changed into a woman. Seven years later, he became a mag again when he saw the same snakes in the same place. In Book III of Ovid's *Metamorphoses*, Tiresias is called to judge a debate between Zeus and Hera. Tiresias supported Zeus and asserted that women had the most pleasure in sex for which Hera cursed him with blindness. Athena blessed him with prophecy as she could not reverse the curse. Zeus gave him a long lifespan of seven hundred years. Tiresias also appears in Homer's *Odyssey* where he gives appropriate instructions to the hero to reclaim his home.

9. Semiramis - legendary Queen of Assyria and founder of Babylon who is said to have led military campaigns and initiated large construction projects.

10. Ninus - the founder of Nineveh (modern-day Mosul, Iraq); he fell in love with Semiramis and married her.

11. Phorcys - a primordial sea deity; son of Pontus and Gaia; father of the gorgons

12. Tartaros - the deepest part of the Underworld reserved for unforgivable sinners; a prison for the fallen Titans; also a primordial deity who gave birth to the Universe.

13. Arethusa - a nymph in the company of Artemis; beloved by the river deity Alpheus; she changed into a fountain and mingled with the waters of Alpheus

14. Amphion - son of Zeus and Antiope; a talented musician taught by Hermes; husband of Niobe; builder of Thebes.

15. Pleiades - seven sisters; companions of Artemis; they later became a constellation.

16. Atlas - son of Iapetus and Clymene; brother of

Prometheus and Epimetheus; he was condemned by Zeus to hold the Earth after siding with the Titans during the war between the Titans and the Olympians.

17. Cadmus - Prince of Phoenicia; brother of Europa; a great hero before the days of Hercules; Herodotus credits him with the discovery of the Greek alphabet.

18. Scritch owl - also called Screech Owl, the howl of this bird was considered an ill omen that foreshadowed death; these birds could see ghosts and they were often chosen as familiars by witches and sorcerers.

19. Maenad - female followers of Bacchus/Dionysus, the god of wine and theatre; they became drunk and roamed the deserted streets during Bacchanalia and other rites performed for the god; believed to mutilate and kill anyone who came before them when they were possessed by the god.

20. Circe - legendary sorceress; daughter of the Titan Helios and the nymph Perse; she possessed an inherent talent of transfiguration; she could change humans into animals through powerful drugs and incantations; she was one of the famed trinity of legendary witches along with Pasiphaë and Medea.

21. Siren - a creature, half-woman and half-bird, that lured sailors to death with her melodious voice; Orpheus was the only one who could outwit them in music; Odysseus asked his sailors to block their ear canals with wax when his ship approached their island. He had himself tied around the mast to listen to their songs. He wailed and wept to be released after listening to them but the ship sailed away safely. These sirens were believed to snatch off sailors and eat them alive.

22. Orpheus - legendary musician; son of the muse Calliope; he had the gift of moving rocks and rivers with his

melody; killed by maenads; his lips were still singing even after death; became a constellation.

23. Chthonic - related to the Underworld; also included deities such as Hades, Persephone, Hecate and creatures like Cerberus and the Erinyes/Furies.

24. Twelve Labours of Hercules - a series of trials faced by the hero Hercules to appease the goddess Hera; King Eurystheus gives the trials to cleanse him after he had murdered his wife and children.

25. Moirai - the three goddesses who determined human destiny; they often appeared as weavers with their threads; Clotho was the Spinner who pulled out the thread and determined its quality, Lachesis allotted the length and Atropos cut the thread (the thread being human life)

26. Caduceus - sacred staff carried by Hermes/Mercury; it was believed to be made of olive wood entangled with two snakes in opposite directions and a pair of wings symbolising the speed of Hermes and also his role as a divine messenger.

27. Maia's boy - Hermes/Mercury

28. Amazons - legendary female warriors who surpassed the physical agility, strength and prowess of men; ruled by their Queen Hippolyta, they often launched military expeditions; founders of temples; they supported the Trojans in the Trojan War under their Queen Penthesileia.

29. Prometheus - a Titan; a trickster god and a god of fire; one who introduced the art of sacrifice to humans; tricked Zeus during a sacrifice for which the latter hid fire; Prometheus stole fire from Mt. Olympus and gave it to the humans for which Zeus created Pandora and tricked his brother Epimetheus into marrying her.

30. Saturnia - a title given to Hera/Juno because she was the daughter of Saturn/Chronos

31. Paris - also called Alexandros; son of Priam and Hecuba; Prince of Troy; one who was given Helen by the goddess Aphrodite.

32. Trojan War - a legendary war fought in the 13th century BCE between Greece and Troy (modern-day Hisarlik, Turkey) over the alleged kidnapping of Helen, wife of Menelaus.

33. Muses - the nine goddesses of poetry, astronomy, tragedy and comedy; daughters of Zeus and Mnemosyne (memory); it was customary for all classical epic poets to invoke them preferably in the opening lines of their poems.

34. Naiad - a nymph of flowing water i.e rivers, springs, fountains; they were mortal but had long life spans

35. Shades - spirits of the dead residing in the Underworld, waiting for judgement from the three divine judges

36. Charon - ferryman of the dead; he ferried only those who had been buried with all rituals; the Greeks left coins over the eyes of the dead or in the urns containing the ashes of the dead as a bribe for Charon.

37. Foam-born goddess - a title given to Aphrodite because she rose up from the foam off the island of Cythera; she was born when Chronos threw the genitals of Uranus into the sea.

38. Dryad - also called hamadryad; a nymph who resides in trees and plants; exceptionally beautiful but hostile to humans; they died with the plant

39. Cytherea - another title given to Aphrodite because she was born near the island of Cythera

40. Cybele - an ancient Greco-Roman deity; worshipped by Trojans as an Earth goddess; called 'Mother of the Gods'

by the Romans; born as a hermaphrodite (with both male and female sex organs); she was castrated by the primeval deities because they were afraid of her powers.

41. Agamemnon - King of Mycenae; commander of the Greek contingent in the Trojan War; brother of Menelaus; husband of Clytemnestra; son of Atreus and Aërope; a great warrior but a selfish ruler who wanted to conquer the whole of Asia Minor and expand his territory.

42. Odysseus/Ulysses - hero of Homer's *Odyssey*; king of Ithaca; son of Laërtes and Anticlea; husband of the faithful Penelope; father of Telemachus; known for his wits than his physical prowess; said to have developed the idea of the Trojan Horse and wounded Polyphemus (one-eyed Cyclop son of Poseidon)

43. Ichor - a heavenly fluid that is said to be the blood of the gods; toxic to humans; Diomed was the only human mentioned by Homer to have wounded the goddess Aphrodite and released ichor from her veins; Prometheus' wounds bled ichor when his liver was eaten by an eagle every day

44. Iris - goddess of the rainbow; a minor messenger deity

45. Enyo - a daimon (spirit) of war; equivalent to Bellona, the Roman goddess of war; companion of Ares; Homer credited only Athena and Enyo as companions of heroes

46. Charis - Homer makes her the consort of Hephaestos; one of the three Graces

47. *Aethiopis* - a lost Greek epic; attributed to Arctinus Milesius; said to complete the Trojan War series of epics

48. Hecatombs - an ancient Greek custom of offering a hundred victims in sacrifice to the gods

49. Aegisthus - son of Thyestes and Pelopia (Thyestes' daughter) born as a result of incest. Thyestes and Atreus

were always competing for the throne of Mycenae. Aegisthus killed Atreus so he could jointly rule Mycenae with his father. Agamemnon (son of Atreus) drove him out and reclaimed the throne. To take his vengeance, Aegisthus seduced Agamemnon's wife Clytemnestra in his absence. Aegisthus murdered Agamemnon when he returned to Mycenae after the Trojan War. Aegisthus became king of Mycenae again and ruled for seven years before Orestes (Agamemnon's son) killed him. Thus, it is a who-kills-whose-dad game that went on for centuries much like Zeus, Cronos and their ancestors.

50. Orestes - son of Agamemnon and Clytemnestra; brother of Electra. He murders Aegisthus and his mother Clytemnestra for killing his father. In Aegisthus' *Eumenides*, Orestes goes mad and is chased by the Erinyes or Furies for killing his mother. The Furies exact vengeance on all who kill their own blood. The goddess Athena holds a trial where Orestes says that Apollo commanded him to kill Aegisthus. But Apollo is powerless against the Furies. Athena rescues Orestes and the Furies are converted into Eumenides or goddesses who advise people.

51. Neoptolemus - son of Achilles and Deidamia, the princess of Skyros. Before reaching Troy, Achilles and the Myrmidons conquer Skyros and Achilles marries Deidamia. She had protected him when Thetis hid him with the women in the court of the king of Skyros. Achilles was called Pyrrha then and so his son was also called Pyrrhus. Neoptolemus is a furious warrior and crueller than his father. He sacrifices Polyxena, the last surviving daughter of Priam and Hecuba, over the tomb of Achilles.

52. Orion - the son of Poseidon and Euryale (daughter of

Minos of Crete). He was very popular for his hunting skills and archery. He is said to have hunted with Artemis who killed him by sending a giant scorpion when he tried to rival her. Zeus changed Orion into a constellation and placed him in the sky.

53. Tantalus - a son of Zeus. He was called to a feast by Zeus and he stole ambrosia, the food that makes the gods immortal. Tantalus wanted to make himself and his people immortal. Zeus caught him but forgave him the first time. Then Tantalus invited all the gods to a feast. He cooked his own son Pelops and mixed human meat into the sacrifice to see if the gods could find it. Zeus identified the presence of human meat and punished Tantalus by throwing him into Tartarus, the darkest part of the Underworld. There, Tantalus had to stand in a lake and the water would go down if he tried to drink. All manners of fruit trees grew around him but if he reached out to pluck one, the trees would wither and die.

54. Sisyphus - a prince of Thessaly who fooled death twice. When Hades went ahead to capture Sisyphus' soul with his chains of death, Sisyphus asked him how the chains worked. Hades laid them down to demonstrate and Sisyphus captured Hades with his own chains. Zeus intervened and released Hades as no one died for a long time. The second time Hades came for him, Sisyphus went to the Underworld and told Persephone that he had been wrongly brought there. She released him and he escaped. Finally, Hermes captured him and sent him to Tartarus where he had to roll a huge boulder over a hill. Once he had brought it up, the boulder would roll down and he had to do it all over again.

55. Scylla - daughter of Crataiis or Hecate; she was once a

beautiful nymph who was beloved by Glaucus, the man who became a sea god. Scylla rejected Glaucus' advances and the god went to Circe for help. But Circe lusted after Glaucus and out of jealousy, poured a vial of poison into the rock pool where Scylla bathed. Poor Scylla was transformed into a hideous monster when she bathed in the water.

56. Leucothoe - Ino, the daughter of Cadmus and sister of Semele (mother of Dionysus) was driven insane by Hera. This was because Ino cared for Dionysus, the son of Zeus and Semele. Out of insanity, Ino leaped into the sea. Zeus took pity on her and transformed her into Leucothoe or the goddess of the foam. She is not to be confused with Leucothoe, the beloved of Apollo who became the frankincense tree.

57. Icarius – father of Penelope; brother of Tyndareus (King of Sparta and Helen's father). Icarius was a champion runner who announced that he would marry his daughter to the one who defeated him in a race. Odysseus outran him and married Penelope.

58. Nemesis – goddess of divine retribution; originally she was the goddess of fortune. Later she became the goddess of vengeance brought about by sin or hubris (pride) against the deities. According to Hesiod, she was the daughter of Nyx (primeval deity of night).

Appendix - 1: List Of Greco-roman Deities

1. Zeus/Jupiter/Jove

    King of the Olympian deities, son of Chronos and Rhea, wielder of thunder and lightning, god of leadership, success and strength

2. Hera/Juno

    Queen of the Olympian deities, wife and sister of Zeus, goddess of wealth, fertility and marriage

3. Poseidon/Neptune

    god of the sea, brother of Zeus, husband of Amphitrite

4. Hades/Pluto

    god of the Underworld; brother of Zeus

5. Persephone/Proserpine

    goddess of the Underworld, wife of Hades and daughter of Ceres

6. Athena/Minerva

    goddess of wisdom, art and battle; wielder of the aegis; said to have born from the head of Zeus

7. Ares/Mars

    god of war

8. Ceres/Demeter

    goddess of agriculture; sister of Zeus and Hera

9. Aphrodite/Venus

    Goddess of beauty and love; wife of Hephaestos; mistress of Ares

10. Artemis/Diana/Phoebe

    goddess of the hunt; daughter of Latona (Leta) and Zeus

11. Apollo/Phoebus

god of poetry, music and medicine; son of Latona and Zeus

12. Eros/Cupid

    god of love and sex; son of Aphrodite and Ares

13. Hymen

    god of marriage

14. Hermes/Mercury

    god of communication, travel, trade and commerce; Messenger of the gods

15. Bacchus/Dionysus

    god of wine, revelry, dance and theatre

16. Hephaestos/Vulcan

    god of fire; divine blacksmith (one who forged Zeus' Lightning Bolt, Poseidon's Trident and Hades' Pitchfork); maker of Achilles' shield

17. Hecate

    Tri-faced goddess of magic, herbs, poison and ghosts; adopted by the Greeks but older than the Greek deities; worshipped by the Titans and the Olympians themselves

18. Pan/Faunus

    god of the wild, shepherds and fertility

19. Hestia/Vesta

    goddess of the hearth and home

20. Eris/Discordia

    goddess of strife

21. Nike/Victoria

    goddess of victory

22. Hebe/Juventas

    goddess of youth

23. Tyche/Fortuna

    goddess of luck

24. Janus (Roman)

    god of gates, time and beginnings
25. Pomona (Roman)

    goddess of fruits, wife of Vertumnus
26. Vertumnus (Roman)

    god of seasons
27. Iris/Arcus

    goddess of rainbow
28. Lucina

    goddess of childbirth
29. Ilithyia

    goddess of labour
30. Morpheus/Somnia

    god of sleep
31. Latona

    Titan goddess of fertility; mother of Apollo and Artemis
32. Cybele (Trojan/Asian)

    goddess of earth, the wilds; a hermaphrodite (both male and female); adopted by the Greeks; Mother of the Gods

Primordial Deities

The Primordial deities are first generation gods and goddesses often in charge of creation. They were not worshipped and they were not given human characteristics. They represented the Elementals, the Planetary and the Aethereal. The Olympians were third generation deities descended from these Titans. This table makes use of Hesiod's *Theogony* in listing these deities. These Primordial deities married their siblings and gave birth to the Titans.

1. Chaos

    a genderless great void from which everything was created

2. Thalassa

    goddess of the sea

3. Gaia

    goddess of the earth; mother and wife of Uranus; mother of the Titans, the Cyclopes; she gave birth to Pontus and Ourea without male fertilisation

4. Uranus

    god of the sky

5. Ourea

    god of the mountains

6. Pontus

    god of the sea

7. Tartarus

    god of the deep soil (which later became the Underworld), subterranean zones

8. Nyx

    goddess of night

9. Aether

    genderless deity of light, air

10. Hemera

    goddess of day

11. Eros (not the son of Aphrodite)

    god of love

Titans

The Titans were the children born to the Primordial gods of creation. They were the second-generation deities who gave birth to the Olympians. They were often called giants. They were not worshipped but some of them helped Greek heroes. Some of the Titans married their siblings and gave birth to more deities. This list follows the classification of Hesiod in his *Theogony*.

1. Oceanus
   god of rivers, fountains, seas
2. Tethys
   goddess of streams, clouds, and all freshwater sources; wife of Oceanus - Oceanus and Tethys gave birth to the Oceanids (3000 nymphs) and Potamoi (3000 river gods)
3. Coeus
   god of wisdom and stars
4. Phoebe
   goddess of intellect and prophecy; wife of Coeus - Coeus and Phoebe gave birth to Latona/Leto and Asteria
5. Chronos/Kronos
   god of time, manifestations
6. Rhea
   goddess of fertility; wife of Chronos - The Olympians **(Zeus, Poseidon, Hades, Hestia, Demeter and Hera)** were the offspring of Chronos and Rhea
7. Hyperion
   God of light
8. Theia
   goddess of the sky and vision; wife of Hyperion - their children were Helios, Selene and Eos
9. Crius
   god of constellations; husband of Eurybia - Astraeus, Pallas and Perses were their children
10. Iapetus

god of death; husband of Clymene - Atlas, Menoetius, Prometheus and Epimetheus were their children

11. Themis

goddess of law and order; wife of Zeus (nephew) - The Horae (Hours) and the Moirai (Fates) were their progeny

12. Mnemosyne

goddess of memory; wife of Zeus (nephew) - The Muses were their children

Note: Themis and Mnemosyne were wives of Zeus before Hera

Other Minor Deities

1. **The Moirai** - goddesses of the fates; they appeared as three old women spinning threads; Clotho (she who spun), Lachesis (she who allotted the length) and Atropos (she who cut the thread)

2. **The Horae** - goddesses of the hours; Eunomia (order), Dike (justice) and Eriene (peace)

3. **The Gorgons** - three female monsters who were adopted into Greek myths from Asia; demons who had snakes for hair and could transform anyone who saw them into stone; Stheno, Euryale and Medusa; Medusa was the only mortal gorgon

4. **The Giants** - Cyclopes or one-eyed giants famous among them being i) Polyphemus who was killed by Odysseus ii) Otus and Ephialtes - attempted to climb Mt. Olympus and dethrone Zeus iii) Arges, Brontes and Steropes - assistants of Hephaestos iv) Geryon - slain by Hercules

v) Laestragonians - man-eating giants met by Odysseus and vi) Orion - the giant hunter who is now a constellation

5. **The Furies/Erinyes/Eumenides** - female spirits of vengeance who performed many tasks like punishing the dead in the Underworld, bringing vengeance upon those who failed to keep their oaths or killed their kin; they were born when Chronos castrated his father Uranus to prevent him from having any more children with Gaia; the most popular furies were Allecto (endless anger), Megara (envy) and Tisyphone (vengeance)

6. **The Judges of the Dead** - Aikos (former King of Aegina), Minos (former King of Crete) and Rhadhamanthus (former King of Crete and brother of Minos); Aikos judged the souls of Europeans, Rhadhamanthus judged those of Asia and Minos had the final vote; they were chosen by Hades because of their unshakeable integrity, justice and honesty

7. **The Muses** - goddess of poetry, song, dance and science; i) Calliope - epic poetry ii) Clio - history iii) Euterpe - music iv) Erato - lyric poetry v) Melpomene - tragedy vi) Polyhymnia - sacred poetry vii) Terpsichore - dance viii) Thalia - comedy and ix) Urania - astronomy

(Note: the above are called the Olympian Muses because they were the daughters of Zeus. There were other Muses born to Titans and Apollo too. They have been left out here because they are rarely mentioned in major Greek sources.)

1. **Rivers of the Underworld** - these rivers flow through the Underworld; they personify loss, grief, lamentation and oblivion - all the qualities associated with death; the

most popular rivers are i) Styx - the most important river of the Underworld and often mentioned as a goddess; found at the entrance where Charon the Ferryman ferries the souls over to Hades (in some sources like Ovid's *Metamorphoses*, it is Lake Avernus that lies at the entrance to the Underworld); river of hatred; According to Statius, the river into which Thetis dipped Achilles making him invincible to weapons; the river upon which the most binding of oaths were sworn (if these oaths were broken, the Furies were unleashed to bring ruin and death) ii) Acheron - the river of woe iii) Phlegethon - river of fire; leads into Tartaros (specially designed to punish the worst of sinners) iv) Cocytus - river of lamentation; flows into Tartaros, especially to the area where murderers where punished; said to wail like the murderer's victim during the punishment v) Lethe - river of oblivion/forgetfulness - often mentioned in many sources;

2. **The Erotes** - a group of winged gods who managed the arts of love and sex; they were Aphrodite's favourites who often assisted her; they also played pranks on mortals; the most popular Erotes are i) Anteros (requited love) - son of Aphrodite and Ares ii) Eros - son of Aphrodite and Ares; also called Cupid by the Romans iii) Hedylogos (flattery) iv) Hermaphroditus (bisexual love) - son of Aphrodite and Hermes v) Himeros (unrequited love) vi) Hymen - god of marriage vii) Pothos (desire) and viii) Phthonus (romatic jealousy)

3. **The Hesperides** - the four daughters of the Titan Atlas and the evening star Hesperis; they were named Aigle, Erytheia, Hesperia and Arethusa; they were also called Daughters of the Evening or Nymphs of the West; they tended to Hera's sacred orchard in the West called the

Garden of the Hesperides; their tasks included tending to Hera's sacred tree that bore golden apples, one of which was used by Eris to cause chaos at the wedding of Thetis and Peleus (it was Greek tradition to throw apples upon the newly married couple because these fruits symbolised fertility but Eris used the sacred symbol to cause death and ruin)

4. **The Naiades** - freshwater nymphs; often appeared in the form of beautiful women; daughters of river kings; they were often dangerous; Daphne was a naiad who turned into the laurel to protect herself from Apollo

5. **The Oreades** - mountain nymphs who made up the retinue of Artemis; these nymphs were all female and carried bows, arrows and daggers;; Echo was an Oread who fell in love with Narcissus

6. **The Nereides** - the fifty beautiful daughters of Nereus and Doris (deities of the sea); they made up the retinue of Poseidon and waited upon Amphitrite; guided sailors if summoned properly; they appeared in white with red coral wreaths in their hair and sang melodious songs; they lived in a golden palace under the sea; the most popular nereid was Thetis, mother of Achilles

7. **Anemoi/the Four Winds** - minor winged gods of air who obeyed the storm god Aeolus; sons of Aeolus and Aurora/Eos, the goddess of dawn; they are i) Boreas (Roman: Aquilo) - the North Wind and bringer of cold winter storms ii) Zephyrus (Roman: Favonius) - the West Wind and bringer of spring breezes iii) Notus (Roman: Auster) - the South Wind and bringer of Autumn storms iv) Eurus (Roman: Vulturnus) - the East Wind and bringer of summer storms; the Tower of the Winds in Athens functioned as the world's first meteorological station - the names of these winds are

etched onto the marble clock-tower according to the cardinal directions mentioned above.

8. **The Pleiades** - they were the seven daughters of the Titan Atlas and the Oceanid Pleone; they became constellations; they are i) Maia - eldest of the Pleiades and the mother of Hermes by Zeus; it is said that the month of May sprung from her name ii) Electra - mother of Dardanus by Zeus iii) Taygete iv) Alcyone - mother of Aethusa by Poseidon v) Celaeno vi) Asterope - mother of King Oenomaus by Ares vii) Merope - youngest of the Pleiades; wife of King Sisyphus; she became mortal after marrying Sisyphus

Personifications

These are not gods and goddesses but just personifications of a particular virtue, season, human attribute or feeling.

1. Aura - spirit of the breeze personified as a woman
2. Alastor - spirit of vengeance; often called upon for vengeance in family feuds
3. Deimos - spirit of terror
4. Thanatos - god of strength and resilience
5. Eris - spirit of discord, confusion and chaos
6. Nemesis - goddess of retribution/karma
7. Hypnos - god of sleep
8. Eupheme - spirit of praise
9. Mania - spirit of madness
10. Keres - spirit of violent death
11. Phobos - spirit of panic
12. Nike - goddess of victory

13. Soteria - the Saviour/spirit of deliverance, safety, protection
14. Roma - the city of Rome personified as a goddess
15. Thrasos - spirit of courage
16. Zelos - spirit of rivalry and envy

Appendix 2 - The Creation Myth

Greek mythology is as vast as an ocean; it is a universe of its own. There are diverse versions of these narratives produced by different authors over the centuries. Most of these tales were oral narratives, meant to be sung by a bard over a campfire or in the palace of a king. Later, they were recorded by scribes and scholars who worked in ancient libraries like the one at Alexandria. Many of these scrolls were destroyed in fire and war. We have very few extant texts and all these variations add to the richness of these texts. The 8th century BC was the Golden Age of Greek literature - Hesiod, Homer and many other bards were actively composing their epics during this time.

Greece also adopted written styles from Egypt, Asia and Syria through trade. Sappho predated Homer and Hesiod. She lived during 600 BC and composed more than 1000 poems of which only a few have survived, the best being "Ode to Aphrodite". Sappho was called the "Tenth Muse" and she is the first female classical poet. Aeschylus, Sophocles and Euripides lived even earlier during 400-500 BC. These classical dramatists portray these deities with different attributes. Later writers like Apollodorus, author of the *Bibliotheca* (1st century AD) produced totally different versions.

For brevity and clarity, I have chosen Hesiod's *Theogony* (700 BC?) as the base on which these superstructures are built. Also, *Theogony* is more widely known than other sources and quoted by many classical authors. This is a brief outline of *Theogony* as this vital prose is absolutely essential for the following reasons

i) It is the 'Creation Myth' upon which all other tales are built

ii) Primordial deities and Titans are introduced

iii) The succession myth shows the evolution of the Olympian deities

iv) Greek oral tradition in *Theogony* has been adopted by later poets/minstrels

Why would Hesiod talk about the origin of the gods? Because that's what they wanted. The Muses appeared to him and asked him to do the job. That's what he says as he begins to talk about the Muses.

The Muses

These beautiful goddesses were born in Pereira to Mnemosyne, the goddess of memory and Zeus, the leader of the immortals. They lived on the topmost peaks of Mt. Olympus and had their own castles near those of the Graces. They sang and danced to please the other gods and goddesses. Whoever the Muses favoured most, they bestowed sweet words upon their tongues. The man who was blessed by the Muses (i. e. the poet) was respected and held in awe; the greatest of the kings bowed down to them and he was also called for his straight judgements. Whoever listened to these gifted men (sorry, in those days women were not considered bards though Sappho did the job exceedingly well) soon forgot their worldly troubles.

Chaos and Kronos

Of all the Primordial deities (fundamental powers and forces from which everything was created), the first to be born was Chaos. Then came Gaia (Earth). Eros (love), Erebos and Nyx (night) were born next. Nyx mated with Erebos and gave birth to Aether (air) and Hemera (day). Earth gave birth to Uranus (sky), Ourea (Mountains) and Thalassa (ocean). Gaia mated with Uranus (yes, her son) and gave birth to the Titans - Kronos, Rhea, Oceanus, Tethys, Coeus, Crius, Hyperion, Phoebe, Theia, Iapetus, Mnemosyne, and Themis. Gaia also bore the Cyclopes and three hideous sons 'not to be spoken of' named Kottos, Briareos and Gyges. These three had a hundred arms, and fifty heads and looked so disgusting that their own father hated them. Uranus hid them in a dark cave. There were plenty of other children born to Gaia but Uranus ate them all.

Gaia found out the grisly fate of their children. She pressed the earth and made an adamantine sickle. Let me drop a hint here - Satan and his rebel team are all tied up in adamantine chains in hell in Milton's *Paradise Lost*. So now you see the importance of this text. Gaia called her children (the surviving ones) and asked them who was brave enough to subdue their father. Kronos volunteered. That night, when Uranus desired the love of Gaia, Kronos took the sickle and cut off his father's genitals. The blood splashed everywhere and from these drops, the dreaded Erinyes and the Meliai (tree nymphs) were born.

The genitals fell into the ocean and a white foam grew around them. A goddess was born in this foam and she reached the island of Cythera and then Cypress. The beautiful goddess stepped out of the foam. She was called Aphrodite (she who was born from foam), Cytheria and the Cyprian.

Nyx and the others

Nyx gave birth to Hypnos (sleep), Thanatos (death), Moros (doom), the Moirai (fates), Nemesis (vengeance), Eris (discord) and Erebus (darkness). Nereus gave birth to the fifty Nereids, nymphs of the sea. Ceto and Phorcys became the parents of the Gorgons. Ceto also bore Echidna, a nymph with fair cheeks and curling lashes, half serpent and half woman. Typhaon mated with her and she gave birth to Orthos, the grim Cerberus, the baleful Hydra and the Chimera. Echidna also gave birth to the Sphinx, the Nemean Lion and Ladon (the serpent who guarded the golden apples along with the Hesperides). Tethys mated with Oceanus and gave birth to swirling rivers and the Oceanids. Thea and Hyperion became the parents of Helios (sun), Selene (moon) and Eos (dawn).

Phoebe and Coeus became the parents of Leto (mother of Apollo and Artemis), Asteria and Hecate. Zeus would grant great honours to Hecate making her the most honoured of all the gods. Hecate grants victory to whomever she pleases and she has the right to take it away too. She nurtures children, guides ghosts and guards cattle. Rhea and Kronos gave birth to Hestia, Demeter, Hera, Hades, Poseidon and Zeus. Just like Uranus, Kronos started eating his own children because he was afraid they might subdue him. Rhea took Zeus to Crete and reared him in a cave. She wrapped a boulder in a cloth and showed it to Kronos who immediately swallowed it without even looking at the child. Zeus grew up quickly into a powerful god and stood up against Kronos. After defeating Kronos, Zeus set his father's brothers free and they gave Zeus the power to wield the thunder.

Prometheus

Prometheus was the Titan god of fire, the son of Iapetus and Clymene. He was also hailed as the Champion of Mankind for his constant assistance to men. He was the one who showed men how to offer ritual sacrifices to the gods. But he tricked Zeus the mighty thunderer in the name of a meat sacrifice. One day, Prometheus sacrificed a huge ox, and then he divided the meat and bones into two portions. He took the bones and wrapped them in thin layers of meat for the first portion. Then he took the tough hide and rolled it with the heart, liver and other organs. Zeus came down and saw the trick. Nevertheless, he chose the portion with bones and the thin layer of meat. He was furious when he saw there was nothing but thin layers of meat for him. From that day on, Prometheus had shown man how to offer sacrifices to the gods. Hence you will come across heroes of the *Iliad* and the *Odyssey* wrapping meat around bones and offering them to the gods.

Zeus was angry and took away fire from the humans. Without fire, men could not cook the meat after sacrifice. They could not forge weapons or keep warm during harsh winters. Prometheus stole the immortal fire of the gods in a fennel seed and brought it back to the humans. Zeus was stung with ire when he saw fire dancing forth from the beacons of men. Zeus decided to punish men by sending them the first woman.

Pandora and the Jar of Evils

The name 'Pandora' is not mentioned in *Theogony*. Hesiod continues the Pandora myth in his *Works and Days*. Hephaestos made Pandora from clay following the charming design set by Zeus. Athena dressed her in a gleaming white gown and taught her how to sew. Aphrodite taught her the tricks of love. Hermes taught her deception and cunning. It was Hermes who named her 'Pandora' which meant 'perfect gifts' because all the gods have given her gifts. Finally, Hephaestos also made a golden diadem with all the creatures of the earth and the sea etched upon it. He made it so realistic that the beasts seemed to move in the light. Zeus gave her a jar holding countless plagues that would torture man. (Remember, it is a jar and not a box)

Pandora alighted from Mt. Olympus and wandered the fields among men. Prometheus had warned his brother

Epimetheus not to be fooled by the good looks of the woman. He fell in love with her and took her home. However, he had warned her not to open the jar. Curiosity kills the cat, well, in this case, the woman. She opened it while he was asleep and out flew disease, poverty, jealousy, hatred, anger, greed, gluttony, lust and countless evils. Epimetheus rushed to her and quickly closed the jar. The jar rattled and shook. There was one last thing left in it. That was hope - but Epimetheus had closed the jar shut forever. Hesiod does not mention hope being released into the world.

Zeus had cursed man with woman. Henceforward, all men must succumb to marriage. Those who get good wives must constantly fight between good and evil. Those who get bad wives must live in unrelenting pain in their hearts. Those who choose to live celibate must die alone. That being done, Prometheus did not go free either. Zeus condemned him to eternal punishment. Prometheus was tied up on a ravine, his legs hanging over a deep chasm. An eagle would devour his liver every day. The liver grew back in the evening and the eagle would return the next day. Prometheus endured this punishment till Hercules saved him.

The Titans and the Olympians

The Titans and their children had been quarrelling for over ten years. Only one force could rule the world and Zeus was not going to give up to the Titans. Zeus released Kottos, Briareos and Gyges (his monster uncles) from their cave and added them to his army. The war began and everyone fought - both male and female. The Universe shook with their fight. Zeus unleashed his thunder and lightning. The Titans lost the battle and were forced to recede into Tartaros. If you threw a hammer into Tartaros from earth, it would fall for nine days. Such was the immense foreboding depth of this pit into which all the worst sinners of myth are confined. Poseidon closed the chasm with brazen doors and these are guarded by Kottos, Briareos and Gyges. They were the trusty guardians of Zeus.

The Underworld

The Greek Underworld is separated into Elysium, Tartaros and Avernus. The souls of the dead await the ferryman Charon on the shores of Lake Avernus. The entrance into Avernus is guarded by Cerberus, the triple-headed dog loyal to none but Hades. Hypnos, Thanatos and Morpheus live on Avernus. Upon the edge of Avernus is the castle of Hades where the dead are taken to be judged. The goddess Styx lives nearby; the eldest daughter of Oceanus. Styx is the first river to flow in the Underworld. Zeus has granted Styx a great power. Whoever swears upon the waters of Styx must fulfil his promise. If he fails, he would be denied ambrosia and nectar for a full year. He would lose his status as a god and lie in a coma for nine years. Tartaros is a foul place, grim and dark, full of monsters reserved for the sinners. Elysium is a beautiful garden where the innocent dead would wander forever.

The Children of Zeus

The mighty Zeus decided to enlarge his family. He married Metis, the wisest woman among all gods and men. But when she was about to give birth to Athena, Zeus swallowed her because he thought she would give birth to someone who would dethrone him (like how he did to Kronos and how Kronos dethroned Uranus before). Nevertheless, Athena, fully formed and armoured, jumped out from his head. She is the only one among his children to be born without a mother. Next, Zeus married Themis (justice) who gave birth to the Fates. Then he married Eurynome (daughter of Oceanus) and she gave birth to the Graces.

Zeus went on to marry his sister Demeter (it was common in mythology and ancient history). She gave birth to Persephone. Then Zeus married Mnemosyne from whom the nine Muses were born. Leto gave birth to Apollo and Artemis. Last of all, he married Hera, his sister, the goddess of wealth and fertility. She gave birth to Hebe, Ares, Hephaestos and Ilithyia.

Apart from his wives, Zeus had innumerable lovers among the goddesses, nymphs and mortal women. Maia, the daughter of the Titan Atlas, bore him the god Hermes. Semele bore him the immortal Bacchus. Alcmene gave him Hercules, the renowned hero of Greece.

Poseidon married Amphitrite and she gave birth to Triton. Ares fell in love with Aphrodite and to her was born Harmonia. Helios married the Oceanid Perseïs and she gave birth to Circe and Aeëtes. Cadmus married Harmonia (daughter of Ares and Aphrodite) and she gave birth to Ino, Semele (mother of Bacchus)Agaue and Autonoe. Callirhoe (daughter of Oceanus) married Chrysaor (the man born from the blood of Medusa) and bore Geryoneus, the strongest among all mortals. He was killed by Hercules. Tithonus married fair Aurora and she gave birth to Memnon, king of the Ethiopians. Aphrodite bore Aeneas to Anchises. Circe was intimate with Odysseus and bore Agrius and Latinus from their union. Likewise, Calypso bore Odysseus Nausithous and Nausinous.

References

References

Homer. *The Iliad and the Odyssey*. Translated by Samuel Butler, Fingerprint Classics, 2022.

Ovid. *The Metamorphoses*. Translated by Horace Gregory, Signet Classics, 2009.

Tennyson, Alfred Lord. "Oenone." Poetry Foundation, https://www.poetryfoundation.org/poems/45373/oenone Accessed 12 June 2023.

Virgil. The Aeneid. Translated by Robert Fagles, Penguin Classics, 2006.

Bibliography

Apollodorus. *The Library of Greek Mythology*. Translated by Robin Hard, Oxford University Press, 2008.

Frazer, James George. *The Golden Bough: A Study of Magic and Religion*. Floating Press, 2009.

Hamilton, Edith. *Mythology: Timeless Tales of Gods and Heroes*, Hachette Press, 2011.

Herodotus. *The Histories*. Translated by Andrea L. Purvis, edited by Robert B. Strassler, Anchor, 2009.

Hesiod. *Theogony, Works and Days*. Translated by M. L. West, Oxford University Press, 1988.

Nagy, Gregory. *The Ancient Greek Hero in 24 Hours*. Harvard University Press, 2013.

Napoli, Donna Jo. *Treasury of Greek Mythology: Classic Stories of Gods, Goddesses, Heroes and Monsters*. National Geographic Society, 2011.

Sappho. *Ode to Aphrodite: The Poems and Fragments of Sappho*. Translated by John Myers O'Hara and Henry De Vere Stacpoole, Read Books, 2022.